TWENTIETH CENTURY VIEWS

The aim of this series is to present the best
in contemporary critical opinion on major
authors, providing a twentieth century per-
spective on their changing status in an era
of profound revaluation.

Maynard Mack, *Series Editor*
Yale University

WILLIAM CARLOS WILLIAMS

WILLIAM CARLOS
WILLIAMS

A COLLECTION OF CRITICAL ESSAYS

Edited by

J. Hillis Miller

Prentice-Hall, Inc. *Englewood Cliffs, N. J.*

A SPECTRUM BOOK

The author wishes to thank New Directions Publishing Corporation for permission to use quotations from the following works by William Carlos Williams: *In the American Grain,* copyright © 1925 by James Laughlin, copyright © 1933 by William Carlos Williams; *The Collected Earlier Poems of William Carlos Williams,* copyright © 1938, 1951 by William Carlos Williams; *Many Loves and Other Plays,* copyright © 1936, 1942, and 1948 by William Carlos Williams, copyright © 1961 by Florence Williams; *Pictures from Brueghel and Other Poems,* copyright © 1949, 1951, 1952, 1953, 1954, 1955, 1956, 1957, 1959, 1960, 1961, and 1962 by William Carlos Williams; *The Collected Later Poems of William Carlos Williams,* copyright © 1944, 1948, 1950, and 1963 by William Carlos Williams; *Paterson,* copyright © 1946, 1948, 1949, 1951, and 1958 by William Carlos Williams, copyright © 1963 by Florence Williams; *The Autobiography of William Carlos Williams,* copyright © 1948, 1949, and 1951 by William Carlos Williams; *Selected Essays of William Carlos Williams,* copyright © 1931, 1936, 1938, 1939, 1940, 1942, 1946, 1948, 1949, 1951, and 1954 by William Carlos Williams; and *The Farmers' Daughters: The Collected Stories of William Carlos Williams,* copyright © 1932, 1933, 1934, 1937, 1938, 1941, 1943, 1947, 1949, and 1950 by William Carlos Williams, copyright © 1957 by Florence Williams, copyright © 1961 by New Directions Publishing Corporation.

In addition, the author is grateful to Mrs. Florence H. Williams for permission to use quotations from the following works by William Carlos Williams: *Poems,* privately printed, 1909; *The Great American Novel* (Paris: Contact Editions, 1923), copyright © 1923 by William Carlos Williams, copyright © 1960 by Florence H. Williams; *Spring and All* (Dijon: Contact Publishing Co., 1923), copyrighted by the author.

The author also wishes to thank Ivan Obolensky, Inc., New York, for permission to quote from *Selected Letters of William Carlos Williams,* copyright © 1957 by William Carlos Williams; City Lights Books, San Francisco, for permission to quote from *Kora in Hell: Improvisations,* copyright © 1920 by The Four Seas Company, Boston, copyright © 1957 by Williaam Carlos Williams; and The Beacon Press, Boston, for permission to quote from *I Wanted to Write a Poem: The Autobiography of the Works of a Poet,* reported and edited by Edith Heal (Boston: The Beacon Press, 1958), copyright © 1958 by William Carlos Williams.

Current printing (last number):
10 9 8 7 6 5 4 3 2 1

Preface

This book, as far as I know, is the first collection of essays on William Carlos Williams, though there have been several book-length studies of his work and several more are promised for the near future. The essays I have chosen form a brief history of opinion about Williams' work. In fact, since almost all the critics are Americans, they might be taken as representing, in microcosm, the development of literary taste in America since the '20s.

The first essay after the introduction is by Williams himself and is part of the prose from *Spring and All* (1923). This volume contains two of Williams' most famous poems, "By the road to the contagious hospital" and "The Red Wheelbarrow." These poems cannot be fully understood apart from the context of the prose around them. For some reason, however, this prose has never been reprinted and is available only to those who can see the rare first edition. It contains Williams' most explicit definition of the nature of literature. Here the aesthetics of a poetry of immediacy are clearly worked out. After selections from this important text, the critical essays are placed more or less in chronological order. They go all the way from early essays by Ezra Pound, Marianne Moore, Kenneth Burke, and Wallace Stevens, through a group of studies by university-based critics, to essays by younger poets. The latter testify to Williams' strong influence on the most vital poetry being written in America today. It is possible that Williams, even more than Stevens, say, or Frost, will appear to later eyes as the initiator of a new tradition in literature, the creator of a poetry uniquely American in language and measure. Certainly it was his aim to create such a poetry.

The sequence of the essays presented here also gives evidence of most of Williams' important literary associations, from those with his contemporaries, the poets working side by side with him, to those with the younger poets he has influenced. Yvor Winters has been kind enough to add a postscript bringing the judgment of his essay of 1939 up to date; I have been able to include Kenneth Burke's admirable essay of 1963; and my colleague Richard Macksey has written a study of Williams especially for this volume, as well as allowing me to print here his excellent chronology of Williams'

life and writings. The most notable of Williams' associates not repre-
sented here is Louis Zukofsky, the leader of the "Objectivist" group.
Reference to comments by Zukofsky on Williams may be found in
the bibliography at the end of this volume, and that bibliography
also contains a selected list of further essays and books on Williams.

Quotations from Williams' work in early essays, for example those
by Marianne Moore and Kenneth Burke, were drawn from early
texts of Williams' writing and sometimes differ slightly from the
final versions in the collected volumes. Except in cases of obvious
misprints, I have allowed the quotations to stand in the form in
which they were given, since the critics, after all, were responding
to these versions of Williams' poems. An example of this is the
eighth line of "The Great Figure" as cited by Kenneth Burke. This
line does not appear in the final version of the poem in *The Col-
lected Earlier Poems.*

Richard Macksey has been of great assistance in lending me books
by and about Williams and in helping me track down obscure
essays. I wish to thank Mr. James Laughlin and Mrs. Florence H.
Williams for their generous help. I wish also to thank the staff of
the Milton S. Eisenhower Library at Johns Hopkins and to express
my gratitude to Mr. Donald Gallup and the staff of the Beinecke
Library at Yale for making available to me the Williams collection
there.

Contents

Introduction

by J. Hillis Miller

William Carlos Williams was born in Rutherford, New Jersey, in 1883. After medical training at the University of Pennsylvania, he spent the rest of his life, until his retirement in 1951, practicing medicine in Rutherford. He met Ezra Pound at the University of Pennsylvania, and later came to know Marianne Moore, Wallace Stevens, Louis Zukofsky, and other poets and artists. During a long lifetime he published several dozen books—poems, plays, stories, novels, essays, a book about American history, an autobiography. The complete body of his published poetry, with a few unimportant omissions, may be read in four volumes: *The Collected Earlier Poems, The Collected Later Poems, Paterson,* and *Pictures from Brueghel.* He died in 1963 at the age of seventy-nine.[1]

Though Williams' work received considerable attention during his lifetime, he has only gradually come to be recognized as one of the most important of twentieth century American poets, one deserving a place beside Pound, Eliot, Frost, and Stevens. His work registers a change in sensibility which puts him, along with other writers in America and abroad, beyond the characteristic assumptions of romanticism. Since these assumptions have for the most part been dominant in Western literature since the late eighteenth century, full understanding of Williams' work has been slow to develop. Though there is a recognizable kinship between that work and the work of certain other poets, artists, and philosophers of the twentieth century, Williams' presuppositions about poetry and human existence are his own. They are a unique version of a new tradition. What they are and the way they are implicit in each of his poems can only be discovered by that immersion in his writing which must precede interpretation of any part of it.

---

[1] See the chronology at the end of this volume for fuller information about Williams' life and for a complete list of his publications in book form. The various volumes of Williams' poetry are now being published in England by MacGibbon & Kee Ltd.

The difficulties of such interpretation may be suggested by consideration of the ways Williams' work fails to provide the reader habituated to romantic or symbolist poetry with the qualities he expects. Like a late eighteenth century reader encountering the *Lyrical Ballads,* many present-day readers of Williams "will look round for poetry, and will be induced to inquire by what species of courtesy these attempts can be permitted to assume that title." [2] Here is a characteristic text from "Collected Poems 1934":

Young Sycamore

I must tell you
this young tree
whose round and firm trunk
between the wet

pavement and the gutter
(where water
is trickling) rises
bodily

into the air with
one undulant
thrust half its height—
and then

dividing and waning
sending out
young branches on
all sides—

hung with cocoons
it thins
till nothing is left of it
but two

eccentric knotted
twigs
bending forward
hornlike at the top[3]

[2] Wordsworth's phrasing, in the preface to *Lyrical Ballads* (*The Poetical Works of William Wordsworth,* ed. E. de Selincourt, II [London: Oxford University Press, 1952], 386).

[3] The following texts of Williams' work have been used in this Introduction. Each is accompanied by the abbreviaton which will hereafter be employed in

Such a poem seems recalcitrant to analysis. The sycamore is not a symbol. "No symbolism is acceptable," says the poet (SE, 213). The tree does not stand for anything, or point to anything beyond itself. Like the red wheelbarrow, or the sea-trout and butterfish, or the flowering chicory in other poems by Williams, the young sycamore is itself, means itself. It is an object in space, separated from other objects in space, with its own sharp edges, its own innate particularity. The tree stands "between" the pavement and the gutter, but there is no assertion of an interchange between the three objects, no flow of an ubiquitous nature-spirit binding all things together. Things for Williams exist side by side in the world, and the poet here locates the sycamore by reference to the things closest to it.

The avoidance of symbolism in Williams' poetry is related to the absence of another quality—the dimension of depth. In romantic poetry, space frequently leads out to a "behind" or "beyond" which the poet may reach through objects, or which objects signify at a distance. In the Christian and Platonic traditions, things of this world in one way or another stand for things of the other world. Romantic poets inherit or extend this tradition, as in the thoughts too deep for tears which for Wordsworth are given by the meanest flower that blows, or as in the attraction of the "Far-far-away" for Tennyson, or as in Yeats's reaffirmation of the hermetic tradition in "Ribh denounces Patrick": "For things below are copies, the Great Smaragdine Tablet said." In Williams' poetry this kind of depth has disappeared and with it the symbolism appropriate to it. Objects for him exist within a shallow space, like that created on the canvases of the American abstract expressionists. "Anywhere is everywhere" (P, 273), and there is no lure of distances which stretch out beyond what can be immediately seen. Nothing exists but what stands just before the poet's wide-awake senses, and "Heaven seems frankly impossible" (SL, 147).

For this reason there is no need to go anywhere or do anything

citations. KH—*Kora in Hell: Improvisations* (San Francisco: City Lights, 1957); SA—*Spring and All* (Dijon: Contact Publishing Company, 1923); IAG—*In the American Grain* (New York: New Directions Publishing Corporation, 1956); CEP—*The Collected Earlier Poems* (New York: New Directions Publishing Corporation, 1951); A—*The Autobiography of William Carlos Williams* (New York: Random House, 1951); SE—*Selected Essays* (New York: Random House, 1954); SL—*Selected Letters,* ed. John C. Thirlwall (New York: Ivan Obolensky, Inc., 1957); ML—*Many Loves and Other Plays* (New York: New Directions Publishing Corporation, 1961); *Pictures from Brueghel and Other Poems* (New York: New Directions Publishing Corporation, 1962); CLP—*The Collected Later Poems* (New York: New Directions Publishing Corporation, 1963); P—*Paterson* (New York: New Directions Publishing Corporation, 1963). "Young Sycamore" is from CEP, 332.

to possess the plenitude of existence. Each of Williams' poems, to borrow the title of one of them, is "the world contracted to a recognizable image" (PB, 42). The poet has that power of "seeing the thing itself without forethought or afterthought but with great intensity of perception" which he praises in his mother (SE, 5), and all his poems have the quality which he claims for "Chicory and Daisies": "A poet witnessing the chicory flower and realizing its virtues of form and color so constructs his praise of it as to borrow no particle from right or left. He gives his poem over to the flower and its plant themselves" (SE, 17). While a poem lasts nothing exists beyond it—nothing but the chicory, in one poem, or bits of broken glass on cinders, in another, or the young sycamore between pavement and gutter in another. Immediacy in space, and also immediacy in time. The present alone is, and the aim of a poem must therefore be "to refine, to clarify, to intensify that eternal moment in which we alone live" (SA, 3). "Young Sycamore" is written in the present tense. It records the instant of Williams' confrontation of the tree.

There can also be for Williams little figurative language, little of that creation of a "pattern of imagery" which often unifies poems written in older traditions. Metaphors compare one thing to another and so blur the individuality of those things. For Williams the uniqueness of each thing is more important than any horizontal resonances it may have with other things: "Although it is a quality of the imagination that it seeks to place together those things which have a common relationship, yet the coining of similes is a pastime of very low order, depending as it does upon a nearly vegetable coincidence. Much more keen is that power which discovers in things those inimitable particles of dissimilarity to all other things which are the peculiar perfections of the thing in question" (SE, 16). "Young Sycamore" contains a single figurative word, "hornlike," and though this word is of great importance in the poem, spreading its implications backward to pick up the overtones of words like "bodily" or "thrust" and suggesting that the sycamore has an animal-like volition and power (or perhaps, as Wallace Stevens has said, the lithe sinuosity of a snake), nevertheless the personification is attenuated. The poem is made chiefly of a long clause which in straightforward language describes the tree from trunk to topmost twig.

Such poetry provides problems not only for the analytical critic, but also for a reader concerned about the uses of poetry. Poetry of the romantic and symbolist traditions is usually dramatic or dialectical in structure. It often presupposes a double division of existence. The objects of this world are separated from the supernatural realities they signify, and the consciousness of the poet is separated both from objects and from their celestial models. A poetry based on such assumptions will be a verbal act bringing about a change in man's relation to the world. In uniting subject and object it will give the poet momentary possession of that distant reality the object symbolizes. Such a poetry is the enactment of a journey which may take the poet and his reader to the very bourne of heaven. Mallarmé's work provides a symbolist version of this poetry of dramatic action. He must avoid at any cost that direct description Williams so willingly accepts, and writes a poetry of indirection in which the covert naming of things is the annihilation of those things so that they may be replaced, beyond negation, by an essence which is purely notional, an aroma "absent from all bouquets."

Nothing of this sort happens in Williams' poetry. "Young Sycamore" does not go anywhere or accomplish any new possession of the tree. There is no gradual approach of subject and object which leads to their merger in an ecstatic union. The reader at the end is where he was at the beginning—standing in imagination before the tree. The sycamore and the poem about the sycamore are separate things, side by side in the world in the same way that the tree stands between the pavement and the gutter without participating in either. Romantic and symbolist poetry is usually an art of willed transformation. In this it is, like science or technology, an example of that changing of things into artifacts which assimilates them into the human world. Williams' poetry, on the other hand, is content to let things be. A good poet, he says, "doesn't *select* his material. What is there to select? It *is*." [4]

No symbolism, no depth, no reference to a world beyond the world, no pattern of imagery, no dialectical structure, no interaction of subject and object—just description. How can the critic "analyze" such a poem? What does it mean? Of what use is it? How can the poet justify the urgency of his first line: "I must tell you"? If the poem does not make anything happen, or give the reader something he did not have before, it seems of no more use than a photograph of the tree.

The answers to these questions can be given only if the reader places himself within the context of the assumptions which underlie the poem. Anywhere is everywhere for Williams not because all places are indifferent, so that one place is as good as another, each one confessing the same failure of mind, objects, and their meanings

[4] Introduction to Byron Vazakas, *Transfigured Night* (New York: The Macmillan Company, 1946), p. xi.

to become one. Quite the opposite is the case. His poetry can give itself to calm description because all objects are already possessed from the beginning, in what he calls an "approximate co-extension with the universe" (SA, 27). The co-extension need be only approximate because that concentration on a single object or group of objects so habitual to Williams confirms his identification with all things. In order to attain that concentration, other things, for the moment, must be set aside; but they are no less there, no less latently present in the realm of co-extension the poet has entered. A primordial union of subject and object is the basic presupposition of Williams' poetry.

In assuming such a union his work joins in that return to the facts of immediate experience which is a widespread tendency in twentieth century thought and art. This tendency may be identified in painters from Cézanne through cubism to abstract expressionism. It may be seen in poets like René Char, Jorge Guillén, Charles Olson, and Robert Creeley. It is visible in that transformation of fiction which has, most recently, generated the French "new novel," the *romans blancs* of Alain Robbe-Grillet or Nathalie Sarraute. It may be found in the linguistic philosophy of Wittgenstein in the *Philosophical Investigations,* and in the tradition of phenomenology from Husserl through Heidegger and Merleau-Ponty. Williams' poetry has its own unique structure and assumptions, but if any milieu is needed for it, this new tradition is the proper one. Though he understood the connection between his work and modern painting, and though he admired, for example, the poetry of Char, the similarities between his writing and other work should not be thought of in terms of "influences." The similarities are rather a matter of independent responses to a new experience of life.

Williams differs from other recent English and American poets in the timing of his acceptance of the new relation to the world. Yeats, Eliot, and Stevens, for example, also move beyond dualism, but this movement fills the whole course of their lives. It is accomplished only in their last work—in the explosive poetry of the moment in Yeats's "High Talk" or "News for the Delphic Oracle," or in the poetry of Incarnation in Eliot's "Four Quartets," or in the fluid improvisations, joining imagination and reality, of Stevens' "An Ordinary Evening in New Haven." Williams, however, begins his career with the abandonment of his separate ego. Only in the unfinished narrative poem written during his medical studies[5] and in his first published volume, the *Poems* of 1909, does he remain

[5] See the *Autobiography,* pp. 59, 60, for his description of this poem.

within the romantic tradition. Themes of spatial distance and of the isolation of the self are dominant there. With his next long poem, "The Wanderer," Williams takes the step beyond romanticism. The poem ends with the protagonist's plunge into the "filthy Passaic." He is swallowed up by "the utter depth of its rottenness" until his separate existence is lost, and he can say, "I knew all—it became me" (CEP, 12). This "interpenetration, both ways" (P, 12) is assumed in all Williams' later poetry. His situation may be defined as "the mind turned inside out" into the world (KH, 72), or, alternatively, as the world turned inside out into the mind, for in the union of poet and river both his separate ego and the objective world disappear. An important letter to Marianne Moore describes this union of inner and outer and the "security" which resulted from it. It is, he says, "something which occurred once when I was about twenty, a sudden resignation to existence, a despair—if you wish to call it that, but a despair which made everything a unit and at the same time a part of myself. I suppose it might be called a sort of nameless religious experience. I resigned, I gave up" (SL, 147).

"Young Sycamore," like the rest of Williams' mature poetry, is written on the basis of this act of resignation. In the poem there is neither subject nor object, but a single realm in which all things are both subjective and objective at once: the tree, the pavement, the gutter, the poem, the poet. The reader is included too, the "you" of the first line. The poet's address to the reader assimilates him into the realm of interpenetration in what Williams calls "a fraternal embrace, the classic caress of author and reader" (SA, 3). In Williams' poetry there is no description of private inner experience. There is also no description of objects which are external to the poet's mind. Nothing is external to his mind. His mind overlaps with things; things overlap with his mind. For this reason "Young Sycamore" is without dramatic action and can limit itself to an itemizing of the parts of the tree. There is no need to do anything to possess the tree because it is already possessed from the beginning.

The imaginary space generated by the words of "Young Sycamore" is not that space of separation, primarily optical, which the reader enters, for example, in the poetry of Matthew Arnold. The poem creates a space appropriate to the more intimate senses whereby the body internalizes the world. Such a space is characterized by intimacy and participation. It denies the laws of geometrical space, in which each thing is in one place and is limited by its surfaces. So Williams describes, for example, that aural space in which each sound permeates the whole world, like the pervasive tone in "The Desert Music" which is everywhere at once, "as when Casals struck/and held a deep cello tone" (PB, 119). Or in "Queen-Ann's-Lace" he experiences a woman and a field of the white flower not as metaphors of one another, but as interpenetrating realities. The poet's body, for Williams, is the place where subject and object are joined, and so, in "Young Sycamore," the tree is described as though its life were taking place inside his own life. The poem is a characteristic example of Williams' minimizing of eyesight and his emphasis on the more intimate senses, hearing, tasting, smelling, and above all touch, that *tactus eruditus* (CEP, 63) which it is proper for a physician to have. The assimilation of the world by the senses makes of the body a kinesthetic pantomime of the activity of nature. "A thing known," says Williams, "passes out of the mind into the muscles" (KH, 71). "Young Sycamore" affirms this possession not only in the tactile imagery of "round and firm trunk" and "bodily," but also in the pattern of verbs or verbals which makes up the framework of the poem: "rises," "undulant/thrust," "dividing and waning," "sending out," "hung," "thins," "knotted," "bending." These words articulate the way the poet lives the life of the tree.

The sequence of verbal forms also expresses the special way in which "Young Sycamore" takes place in a single moment. The instant for Williams is a field of forces in tension. In one sense his poetry is static and spatial. The red wheelbarrow, the locust tree in flower, the young sycamore, even all the things named in long poems like *Paterson* or "Asphodel, That Greeny Flower," stand fixed in the span of an instant. It is therefore appropriate that Book Five of *Paterson,* for example, should be organized according to the spatial image of a tapestry. Nevertheless, there is in every moment a dynamic motion. "Young Sycamore" exemplifies one of the most important modes of this in Williams' poetry: flowering or growth. According to the cosmology of three elements which underlies Williams' poetry,[6] things rise from the "unfathomable ground/ where we walk daily" (CLP, 23), take form in the open, and in that openness uncover a glimpse of the "hidden flame" (IAG, 204), the universal beauty each formed thing both reveals and hides. This revelation takes place only in the process of growing, not in the thing full grown. For Williams the momentary existence even of a static thing like a wheelbarrow contains future and past as ho-

[6] For a description of this elemental cosmology see pp. 328-36 of my essay on Williams in *Poets of Reality: Six Twentieth-Century Writers* (Cambridge, Mass.: Harvard University Press, 1965).

rizons of the present. In its reaching out toward them it reveals the presence of things present, that "strange phosphorus of the life" (IAG, [vii]). His poetry is not primarily spatial. Time, for him, is the fundamental dimension of existence. The dynamic motion of the present creates space, unfolding it in the energy which brings form out of the ground so that it may, for the moment, reveal the "radiant gist" (P, 133). Though the young sycamore is all there in the instant, from trunk to topmost twig, the poet experiences this stasis as a growth within the moment. It is an "undulant thrust" taking the tree up out of the dark ground as a bodily presence which pushes on into the air, "dividing and waning," until it thins out in the last two eccentric knotted twigs bending forward with the aggressive force of horns.

A grammatical peculiarity of the poem may be noted here as a stroke of genius which makes the poem a perfect imitation of the activity of nature. When the undulant thrust from trunk to twigs has been followed to its end the sycamore seems to stand fixed, its energy exhausted, the vitality which urged it into the air now too far from its source in the dark earth. But this is not really true. The inexhaustible force of the temporal thrust of the tree is expressed not only in the cocoons which promise a renewal of the cycle of growth, but also in the fact that there is no main verb in the second clause of the long sentence which makes up the poem. The poem contains so much verbal action that this may not be noticed, but all these verbs are part of a subordinate clause following "whose." Their subject is "trunk" not "tree," and "trunk" is also the apparent referent of "it" in line eighteen. All the movement in the poem takes place within the confines of the subordinate clause. The second line, "this young tree," still hovers incomplete at the end of the poem, reaching out toward the verb which will complement its substantiality with an appropriate action. If the subordinate clause is omitted the poem says: "I must tell you/this young tree"—and then stops. This is undoubtedly the way the poet wanted it. It makes the poem hold permanently open that beauty which is revealed in the tree, just as, in one of Williams' last poems, "Asphodel, That Greeny Flower," the moment of the poem is the endless space of time between a flash of lightning and the sound of thunder:

> The light
> for all time shall outspeed
> the thunder crack.   (PB, 181)

"Young Sycamore" too prolongs indefinitely the moment between

beginning and ending, birth and death. There is, however, a con-
tradiction in what I have said so far about the poem. To say the
poem "expresses" Williams' experience of the temporality of ob-
jects is more or less the same thing as to say it "pictures" or "repre-
sents" or "describes" this. Such a notion presupposes a quadruple
division of existence. The poet is in one place and looks at a tree
which is outside himself. On the basis of his experience of the tree
he makes a poem which mirrors in language his experience. The
reader re-creates the experience through the mediation of the
poem. This is precisely the theory of poetry which Williams em-
phatically denies. Again and again he dismisses the representational
theory of art. Like Charles Olson, he avoids all "pictorial effects"
(ML, 9), all that " 'evocation' of the 'image' which served us for
a time" (SA, 20). Poetry, for him, is "not a mirror up to nature"
(SA, 91), "not a matter of 'representation' " (SA, 45), "nor is it
description nor an evocation of objects or situations" (SA, 91).
The poet must deny such notions of poetry if his writing is to be
true to that union of subject and object he gains with his plunge
into the Passaic. But if the sycamore is already possessed in the
perception of it, of what use is the poem? And yet Williams says
that the aim of poetry is "to repair, to rescue, to complete" (SL,
147). What can this mean? The answer is suggested by another
passage from the letters: "To copy nature is a spineless activity; it
gives us a sense of our mere existence but hardly more than that.
But to imitate nature involves the verb: we then ourselves become
nature, and so invent an object which is an extension of the proc-
ess" (SL, 297). "Young Sycamore" is an object, like the tree itself,
and it grows out of the poet's identification with nature. Like the
tree again, the poem exists as an activity, not as a passive substance.
For this reason it must be a dynamic thing, primarily verbal.

What it means to think of a poem as a thing rather than as a
picture of something is revealed not only by Williams' constant
poetic practice, but, most explicitly, in the prose sections of *Spring
and All* reprinted for the first time in this volume. Words are for
Williams part of the already existing furniture of the world. They
are objects, just as the red wheelbarrow, the bits of green glass, and
the sycamore tree are objects. As a painting is made of paint, or
music of sounds, so a poem is "a small (or large) machine made of
words" (SE, 256). Words differ from bits of green glass or a syca-
more not because meanings are inherent in one case and ascribed
in the other. Both a word and a tree have their meanings as inextri-
cable parts of their substances. But the meaning which is intrinsic to
a word is its power of referring to something beyond itself. Wil-

liams has no fear of the referential power of words. It is an integral part of his theory of imagination. On the one hand he rejects those poets who "use unoriented sounds in place of conventional words" (SA, 92). On the other hand he also rejects the notion that things depend on words. The thing "needs no personal support but exists free from human action" (SA, 91). To think of words as too close to the objects they name would be a return to that kind of description in which "words adhere to certain objects, and have the effect on the sense of oysters, or barnacles" (SA, 90). A further sentence from the prose of *Spring and All* expresses in admirably exact language Williams' way of avoiding these extremes: "The word is not liberated, therefore able to communicate release from the fixities which destroy it until it is accurately tuned to the fact which giving it reality, by its own reality establishes its own freedom from the necessity of a word, thus freeing it and dynamizing it at the same time" (SA, 93).

Here is a concept of poetry which differs both from the classical theory of art as a mirror up to nature and from the romantic theory of art as a lamp radiating unifying light. The word is given reality by the fact it names, but the independence of the fact from the word frees the word to be a fact in its own right and at the same time "dynamizes" it with meaning. The word can then carry the facts named in a new form into the realm of imagination. In this sense poetry rescues and completes. It lifts things up. "Words occur in liberation by virtue of its processes" (SA, 90), but as the words are liberated, so also are the facts they name: "the same things exist, but in a different condition when energized by the imagination" (SA, 75). The words of a poem and the facts they name exist in a tension of attraction and repulsion, of incarnation and transcendence, which is like the relation of dancer and dance. So John of Gaunt's speech in *Richard II* is "a dance over the body of his condition accurately accompanying it" (SA, 91). The poem about the sycamore creates a new object, something "transfused with the same forces which transfuse the earth" (SA, 50). In doing this it affirms its own reality, and it also affirms the independent reality of the tree. The tree is free of the poem, but not free of the poet, for both poem and tree exist with other things in the space of inwardness entered by the poet in his dive into the Passaic. This notion of a free play of words above things, different from them but not detached from them, is expressed concisely in another sentence from *Spring and All*: "As birds' wings beat the solid air without which none could fly so words freed by the imagination affirm reality by their flight" (SA, 91). Bird and air are both real, both equally real, but the bird cannot fly without the air whose solidity it reveals in its flight. So the poem about the sycamore both depends on the tree and is free of it. In its freedom it allows the tree to be itself, at the same time as it confirms its own independent existence.

Now it is possible to see why Williams makes verbs and verb forms the axis of "Young Sycamore." The poem is not a picture of the tree. It is an object which has the same kind of life as the tree. It is an extension of nature's process. In order to be such an object it must have "an intrinsic movement of its own to verify its authenticity" (SE, 257). The pattern of verbs creates this movement. "The poem is made of things—on a field" (A, 333), but words, like other things, exist primarily as energies, directed forces. Words are nodes of linguistic power. This power is their potentiality for combining with other words to form grammatical structures. When words are placed side by side against the white field of the page they interact with one another to create a space occupied by energies in mobile tension.

All Williams' ways with language go to make words act in this way: his rhythmical delicacy, that modulation of words according to the natural measure of breathing which culminates in his development in his last years of the "variable foot"; the separation of words from "greasy contexts" so that, as in the poetry of Marianne Moore, each word stands "crystal clear with no attachments" (SE, 128); the short lines which slow the pace, break grammatical units, and place ordinarily unnoticed words in positions of prominence so that their qualities as centers of linguistic energy may stand out (as in the seventh line of "Young Sycamore," three verbs or verb forms in a row: "is trickling] rises"); the emphasis on the syntax of simple sentences, the "grammatical play" of words which Williams praises in the work of Gertrude Stein (SE, 115). In "Young Sycamore," as in Williams' other poems, each word stands by itself, but is held within the space of the poem by the tension which relates it in undulant motion to the other words. As in the writing of Stein and Laurence Sterne, "The feeling is of words themselves, a curious immediate quality quite apart from their meaning, much as in music different notes are dropped, so to speak, into repeated chords one at a time, one after the other—for themselves alone" (SE, 114). The musical metaphor is important here. The space of the poem is generated by the temporal design of the words. In the time structure of the poem as it is read, as in the tense life of the tree thrusting from trunk to twigs, future and past are held out as horizons of the present in its disclosure.

Poems are more, however, than objects added to the store of objects already existing in nature. The words of a poem "affirm reality by their flight." Language is so natural to man and so taken for granted as part of his being that it is difficult to imagine what the world would be like without it. Though man is not human if he is completely bereft of speech, his language may become soiled or corrupted. Then it will no longer affirm reality, but hide it. It will become part of the "constant barrier between the reader and his consciousness of immediate contact with the world" (SA, 1). The theme of the degradation of language runs all through Williams' writing, from the prose of *Spring and All* and *The Great American Novel* through the analysis of American civilization in *In the American Grain* to the passages on the speech of urban man in *Paterson*: "The language, the language/fails them" (P, 20). Even though man's language is corrupt, the sycamore will still be there and will still be a revelation of beauty. The failure of language, however, means necessarily a failure of man's power to perceive the tree and share its life. The loss of a proper language accompanies man's detachment from the world and from other people. Authentic speech sustains man's openness to the world. It is in this sense that "we smell, hear and see with words and words alone, and . . . with a new language we smell, hear and see afresh" (SE, 266). As Williams puts it in a phrase, the poem alone "focuses the world" (SE, 242).

Language is the unique power man has to bring beauty out of hiding and in so doing to lift up, to repair, to rescue, to complete: "Only the made poem, the verb calls it/into being" (PB, 110). The radiant gist is present in the young sycamore, not projected there by the poet, but it is hidden from most men, for the language fails them. The poet's language brings into the open the revelation which is going on secretly everywhere. It uncovers the presence of things present. This presence inheres in things and in other people, and it also inheres in our speech: "It is actually there, in the life before us, every minute that we are listening, a rarest element— not in our imaginations but there, there in fact. It is that essence which is hidden in the very words which are going in at our ears and from which we must recover underlying meaning as realistically as we recover metal out of ore" (A, 362).

These sentences define exactly Williams' aim as a poet: the attempt through a purification and renewal of language to uncover that rarest element which dwells obscured in the life before us. This notion of the function of poetry justifies the urgency of the first line of "Young Sycamore": "I must tell you." Only in proper language does man's interpenetration with the world exist, and therefore the poet *must* speak. The poem does not make anything happen or transform things in any way. When it is over the tree still stands tranquilly between the wet pavement and the gutter. But in letting the sycamore be, the poem brings it into existence for the reader, through the words, in that caress of intimacy which the first line affirms.

The essays which follow, after the essential passages from the prose of *Spring and All,* show Williams' readers responding in their various ways to his revelation of that beauty which, to borrow a phrase from Wallace Stevens, is his "inescapable and ever-present difficulty and inamorata."

Prose from *Spring and All*

by William Carlos Williams

If anything of moment results—so much the better. And so much the more likely will it be that no one will want to see it.

There is a constant barrier between the reader and his consciousness of immediate contact with the world. If there is an ocean it is here. Or rather, the whole world is between: Yesterday, tomorrow, Europe, Asia, Africa,—all things removed and impossible, the tower of the church at Seville, the Parthenon.

What do they mean when they say: "I do not like your poems; you have no faith whatever. You seem neither to have suffered nor, in fact, to have felt anything very deeply. There is nothing appealing in what you say but on the contrary the poems are positively repellant. They are heartless, cruel, they make fun of humanity. What in God's name do you mean? Are you a pagan? Have you no tolerance for human frailty? Rhyme you may perhaps take away but rhythm! why there is none in your work whatever. Is this what you call poetry? It is the very antithesis of poetry. It is antipoetry. It is the annihilation of life upon which you are bent. Poetry that used to go hand in hand with life, poetry that interpreted our deepest promptings, poetry that inspired, that led us forward to new discoveries, new depths of tolerance, new heights of exaltation. You moderns! it is the death of poetry that you are accomplishing. No. I cannot understand this work. You have not yet suffered a cruel blow from life. When you have suffered you will write differently?"

Perhaps this noble apostrophe means something terrible for me, I am not certain, but for the moment I interpret it to say: "You

From *Spring and All* (Dijon: Contact Publishing Company, 1923), by William Carlos Williams, pp. 1-4, 26-30, 34-38, 41-45, 48-51, 67, 68, 86, 90-93, with omission of some passages on these pages. A few obvious misprints have been corrected. Otherwise the peculiarities of the original text have been retained. Copyright © 1923 by William Carlos Williams. Reprinted by permission of Mrs. Florence H. Williams.

have robbed me. God, I am naked. What shall I do?"—By it they mean that when I have suffered (provided I have not done so as yet) I too shall run for cover; that I too shall seek refuge in fantasy. And mind you, I do not say that I will not. To decorate my age.

But today it is different.

The reader knows himself as he was twenty years ago and he has also in mind a vision of what he would be, some day. Oh, some day! But the thing he never knows and never dares to know is what he is at the exact moment that he is. And this moment is the only thing in which I am at all interested. Ergo, who cares for anything I do? And what do I care?

I love my fellow creature. Jesus, how I love him: endways, sideways, frontways and all the other ways—but he doesn't exist! Neither does she. I do, in a bastardly sort of way.

To whom then am I addressed? To the imagination.

In fact to return upon my theme for the time nearly all writing, up to the present, if not all art, has been especially designed to keep up the barrier between sense and the vaporous fringe which distracts the attention from its agonized approaches to the moment. It has been always a search for "the beautiful illusion." Very well. I am not in search of "the beautiful illusion."

And if when I pompously announce that I am addressed—To the imagination—you believe that I thus divorce myself from life and so defeat my own end, I reply: To refine, to clarify, to intensify that eternal moment in which we alone live there is but a single force—the imagination. This is its book. I myself invite you to read and to see.

In the imagination, we are from henceforth (so long as you read) locked in a fraternal embrace, the classic caress of author and reader. We are one. Whenever I say "I" I mean also "you." And so, together, as one, we shall begin.

*   *   *

The inevitable flux of the seeing eye toward measuring itself by the world it inhabits can only result in himself crushing humiliation unless the individual raise[1] to some approximate co-extension

---

[1] Should "himself" in the previous line follow "raise"? The sentence would then read: ". . . in crushing humiliation unless the individual raise himself. . . ." [Ed.]

with the universe. This is possible by aid of the imagination. Only through the agency of this force can a man feel himself moved largely with sympathetic pulses at work—

A work of the imagination which fails to release the senses in accordance with this major requisite—the sympathies, the intelligence in its selective world, fails at the elucidation, the alleviation which is—
In the composition, the artist does exactly what every eye must do with life, fix the particular with the universality of his own personality—Taught by the largeness of his imagination to feel every form which he sees moving within himself, he must prove the truth of this by expression.

The contraction which is felt.

All this being anterior to technique, that can have only a sequent value; but since all that appears to the senses on a work of art does so through
        fixation by the imagination of the external as well as internal means of expression the essential nature of technique or transcription.

Only when this position is reached can life proper be said to begin since only then can a value be affixed to the forms and activities of which it consists.

Only then can the sense of frustration which ends. All composition defeated.

Only through the imagination is the advance of intelligence possible, to keep beside growing understanding.

Complete lack of imagination would be the same at the cost[2] of intelligence, complete.

Even the most robust constitution has its limits, though the Roman feast with its reliance upon regurgitation to prolong it shows an active ingenuity, yet the powers of a man are so pitifully small, with the ocean to swallow—that at the end of the feast nothing would be left but suicide.

That or the imagination which in this case takes the form of humor, is known in that form—the release from physical necessity.

[2] Should this be "as the loss"? [ED.]

Having eaten to the full we must acknowledge our insufficiency since we have not annihilated all food nor even the quantity of a good sized steer. However we have annihilated all eating: quite plainly we have no more appetite. This is to say that the imagination has removed us from the banal necessity of bursting ourselves —by acknowledging a new situation. We must acknowledge that the ocean we would drink is too vast—but at the same time we realize that extension in our case is not confined to the intestine only. The stomach is full, the ocean no fuller, both have the same quality of fullness. In that, then, one is equal to the other. Having eaten, the man has released his mind.

THIS catalogue might be increased to larger proportions without stimulating the sense.

In works of the imagination that which is taken for great good sense, so that it seems as if an accurate precept were discovered, is in reality not so, but vigor and accuracy of the imagination alone. In work such as Shakespeare's—

This leads to the discovery that has been made today—old catalogues aside—full of meat—

"the divine illusion has about it that inaccuracy which reveals that which I mean."

There is only "illusion" in art where ignorance of the bystander confuses imagination and its works with cruder processes. Truly men feel an enlargement before great or good work, an expansion but this is not, as so many believe today a "lie," a stupefaction, a kind of mesmerism, a thing to block out "life," bitter to the individual, by a "vision of beauty." It is a work of the imagination. It gives the feeling of completion by revealing the oneness of experience; it rouses rather than stupefies the intelligence by demonstrating the importance of personality, by showing the individual, depressed before it, that his life is valuable—when completed by the imagination. And then only. Such work elucidates—

Such a realization shows us the falseness of attempting to "copy" nature. The thing is equally silly when we try to "make" pictures—

But such a picture as that of Juan Gris, though I have not seen it in color, is important as marking more clearly than any I have seen what the modern trend is: the attempt is being made to separate things of the imagination from life, and obviously, by using the forms common to experience so as not to frighten the onlooker away but to invite him,

*   *   *

things with which he is familiar, simple things—at the same time to detach them from ordinary experience to the imagination. Thus they are still "real," they are the same things they would be if photographed or painted by Monet, they are recognizable as the things touched by the hands during the day, but in this painting they are seen to be in some peculiar way—detached

Here is a shutter, a bunch of grapes, a sheet of music, a picture of sea and mountains (particularly fine) which the onlooker is not for a moment permitted to witness as an "illusion." One thing laps over on the other, the cloud laps over on the shutter, the bunch of grapes is part of the handle of the guitar, the mountain and sea are obviously not "the mountain and sea," but a picture of the mountain and the sea. All drawn with admirable simplicity and excellent design—all a unity—

This was not necessary where the subject of art was not "reality" but related to the "gods"—by force or otherwise. There was no need of the "illusion" in such a case since there was none possible where a picture or a work represented simply the imaginative reality which existed in the mind of the onlooker. No special effort was necessary to cleave where the cleavage already existed.

I don't know what the Spanish see in their Velásquez and Goya but

Today where everything is being brought into sight the realism of art has bewildered us, confused us and forced us to re-invent in order to retain that which the older generations had without that effort.

Cézanne—

The only realism in art is of the imagination. It is only thus that the work escapes plagiarism after nature and becomes a creation

Invention of new forms to embody this reality of art, the one thing which art is, must occupy all serious minds concerned.

*   *   *

The great furor about perspective in Holbein's day had as a consequence much fine drawing, it made coins defy gravity, standing on the table as if in the act of falling. To say this was lifelike must have been satisfying to the master, it gave depth, pungency.

But all the while the picture escaped notice—partly because of the perspective. Or if noticed it was for the most part because one could see "the birds pecking at the grapes" in it.

Meanwhile the birds were pecking at the grapes outside the window and in the next street Bauermeister Kummel was letting a gold coin slip from his fingers to the counting table.

The representation was perfect, it "said something one was used to hearing" but with verve, cleverly.

Thus perspective and clever drawing kept the picture continually under cover of the "beautiful illusion" until today, when even Anatole France trips, saying: "Art—all lies!"—today when we are beginning to discover the truth that in great works of the imagination A CREATIVE FORCE IS SHOWN AT WORK MAKING OBJECTS WHICH ALONE COMPLETE SCIENCE AND ALLOW INTELLIGENCE TO SURVIVE—his picture lives anew. It lives as pictures only can: by their power TO ESCAPE ILLUSION and stand between man and nature as saints once stood between man and the sky—their reality in such work, say, as that of Juan Gris

No man could suffer the fragmentary nature of his understanding of his own life—

Whitman's proposals are of the same piece with the modern trend toward imaginative understanding of life. The largeness which he interprets as his identity with the least and the greatest about him, his "democracy," represents the vigor of his imaginative life.

*   *   *

Understood in a practical way, without calling upon mystic agencies, of this or that order, it is that life becomes actual only when it is identified with ourselves. When we name it, life exists. To repeat physical experiences has no—

The only means he has to give value to life is to recognise it with the imagination and name it; this is so. To repeat and repeat the thing without naming it is only to dull the sense and results in frustration.

this makes the artist the prey of life. He is easy of attack.

I think often of my earlier work and what it has cost me not to have been clear. I acknowledge I have moved chaotically about refusing or rejecting most things, seldom accepting values or acknowledging anything.

because I early recognised the futility of acquisitive understanding and at the same time rejected religious dogmatism. My whole life has been spent (so far) in seeking to place a value upon experience and the objects of experience that would satisfy my sense of inclusiveness without redundancy—completeness, lack of frustration with the liberty of choice; the things which the pursuit of "art" offers—

But though I have felt "free" only in the presence of works of the imagination, knowing the quickening of the sense which came of it, and though this experience has held me firm at such times, yet being of a slow but accurate understanding, I have not always been able to complete the intellectual steps which would make me firm in the position.

So most of my life has been lived in hell—a hell of repression lit by flashes of inspiration, when a poem such as this or that would appear

What would have happened in a world similarly lit by the imagination

*　　*　　*

I find that there is work to be done in the creation of new forms, new names for experience

and that "beauty" is related not to "loveliness" but to a state in which reality plays a part

Such painting as that of Juan Gris, coming after the impressionists, the expressionists, Cézanne—and dealing severe strokes as well to the expressionists as to the impressionists group—points forward to what will prove the greatest painting yet produced.

—the illusion once dispensed with, painting has this problem before it: to replace not the forms but the reality of experience with its own—

up to now shapes and meanings but always the illusion relying on composition to give likeness to "nature"

now works of art cannot be left in this category of France's "lie," they must be real, not "realism" but reality itself—

they must give not the sense of frustration but a sense of completion, of actuality—It is not a matter of "representation"—much may be represented actually, but of separate existence.

enlargement—revivification of values,

* * *

When in the condition of imaginative suspense only will the writing have reality, as explained partially in what precedes—Not to attempt, at that time, to set values on the word being used, according to presupposed measures, but to write down that which happens at that time—

To perfect the ability to record at the moment when the consciousness is enlarged by the sympathies and the unity of understanding which the imagination gives, to practice skill in recording the force moving, then to know it, in the largeness of its proportions—

It is the presence of a

This is not "fit" but a unification of experience

That is, the imagination is an actual force comparable to electricity or steam, it is not a plaything but a power that has been used from the first to raise the understanding of—it is not necessary to resort to mysticism—In fact it is this which has kept back the knowledge I seek—

The value of the imagination to the writer consists in its ability to make words. Its unique power is to give created forms reality, actual existence

This separates

Writing is not a searching about in the daily experience for apt similes and pretty thoughts and images. I have experienced that to my sorrow. It is not a conscious recording of the day's experiences "freshly and with the appearance of reality"—This sort of thing is seriously[3] to the development of any ability in a man, it fastens him down, makes him a—It destroys, makes nature an accessory to the particular theory he is following, it blinds him to his world,—

The writer of imagination would find himself released from observing things for the purpose of writing them down later. He would be there to enjoy, to taste, to engage the free world, not a world which he carries like a bag of food, always fearful lest he drop something or someone get more than he,

A world detached from the necessity of recording it, sufficient to itself, removed from him (as it most certainly is) with which he has bitter and delicious relations and from which he is independent— moving at will from one thing to another—as he pleases, unbound —complete

and the unique proof of this is the work of the imagination not "like" anything but transfused with the same forces which transfuse the earth—at least one small part of them.

Nature is the hint to composition not because it is familiar to us and therefore the terms we apply to it have a least common denominator quality which gives them currency—but because it possesses the quality of independent existence, of reality which we feel in ourselves. It is not opposed to art but apposed to it.

I suppose Shakespeare's familiar aphorism about holding the mirror up to nature has done more harm in stabilizing the copyist tendency of the arts among us than—

the mistake in it (though we forget that it is not S. speaking but an imaginative character of his) is to have believed that the reflection of nature is nature. It is not. It is only a sham nature, a "lie."

Of course S. is the most conspicuous example desirable of the falseness of this very thing.

He holds no mirror up to nature but with his imagination rivals nature's composition with his own.

* A word missing here? "Damaging"; "detrimental"? [Ed.]

He himself becomes "nature"—continuing "its" marvels—if you will

* * *

or better: prose has to do with the fact of an emotion; poetry has to do with the dynamisation of emotion into a separate form. This is the force of imagination.

prose: statement of facts concerning emotions, intellectual states, data of all sorts—technical expositions, jargon, of all sorts—fictional and other—

poetry: new form dealt with as a reality in itself.

The form of prose is the accuracy of its subject matter—how best to expose the multiform phases of its material

the form of poetry is related to the movements of the imagination revealed in words—or whatever it may be—

the cleavage is complete

Why should I go further than I am able? Is it not enough for you that I am perfect?

The cleavage goes through all the phases of experience. It is the jump from prose to the process of imagination that is the next great leap of the intelligence—from the simulations of present experience to the facts of the imagination—

the greatest characteristic of the present age is that it is stale—stale as literature—

To enter a new world, and have there freedom of movement and newness.

I mean that there will always be prose painting, representative work, clever as may be in revealing new phases of emotional research presented on the surface.

But the jump from that to Cézanne or back to certain of the primitives is the impossible.

The primitives are not back in some remote age—they are not BEHIND experience. Work which bridges the gap between the rigidities of vulgar experience and the imagination is rare. It is new, immediate—It is so because it is actual, always real. It is experience dynamized into reality.

*   *   *

Either to write or to comprehend poetry the words must be recognized to be moving in a direction separate from the jostling or lack of it which occurs within the piece.

Marianne's words remain separate, each unwilling to group with the others except as they move in the one direction. This is even an important—or amusing—character of Miss Moore's work.

*   *   *

The imagination uses the phraseology of science. It attacks, stirs, animates, is radio-active in all that can be touched by action. Words occur in liberation by virtue of its processes.

In description words adhere to certain objects, and have the effect on the sense of oysters, or barnacles.

But the imagination is wrongly understood when it is supposed to be a removal from reality in the sense of John of Gaunt's speech in Richard the Second: to imagine possession of that which is lost. It is rightly understood when John of Gaunt's words are related not to their sense as objects adherent to his son's welfare or otherwise but as a dance over the body of his condition accurately accompanying it. By this means of the understanding, the play written to be understood as a play, the author and reader are liberated to pirouette with the words which have sprung from the old facts of history, reunited in present passion.

To understand the words as so liberated is to understand poetry. That they move independently when set free is the mark of their value

Imagination is not to avoid reality, nor is it description nor an evocation of objects or situations, it is to say that poetry does not tamper with the world but moves it—It affirms reality most powerfully and therefore, since reality needs no personal support but exists free from human action, as proven by science in the indestructibility of matter and of force, it creates a new object, a play, a dance which is not a mirror up to nature but—

As birds' wings beat the solid air without which none could fly so words freed by the imagination affirm reality by their flight

Writing is likened to music. The object would be it seems to make poetry a pure art, like music. Painting too. Writing, as with certain of the modern Russians whose work I have seen, would use unoriented sounds in place of conventional words. The poem then would be completely liberated when there is identity of sound with something—perhaps the emotion.

I do not believe that writing is music. I do not believe writing would gain in quality or force by seeking to attain to the conditions of music.

I think the conditions of music are objects for the action of the writer's imagination just as a table or—

According to my present theme the writer of imagination would attain closest to the conditions of music not when his words are disassociated from natural objects and specified meanings but when they are liberated from the usual quality of that meaning by transposition into another medium, the imagination.

Sometimes I speak of imagination as a force, an electricity or a medium, a place. It is immaterial which: for whether it is the condition of a place or a dynamization its effect is the same: to free the world of fact from the impositions of "art" (see Hartley's last chapter[4]) and to liberate the man to act in whatever direction his disposition leads.

The word is not liberated, therefore able to communicate release from the fixities which destroy it until it is accurately tuned to the fact which giving it reality, by its own reality establishes its own freedom from the necessity of a word, thus freeing it and dynamizing it at the same time.

[4] The reference is undoubtedly to Marsden Hartley's *Adventures in the Arts* (New York: Boni and Liveright, 1921). [ED.]

Dr Williams' Position

by Ezra Pound

There is an anecdote told me by his mother, who wished me to understand his character, as follows: The young William Carlos, aged let us say about seven, arose in the morning, dressed and put on his shoes. Both shoes buttoned on the left side. He regarded this untoward phenomenon for a few moments and then carefully removed the shoes, placed shoe *a* that had been on his left foot, on his right foot, and shoe *b*, that had been on the right foot, on his left foot; both sets of buttons again appeared on the left side of the shoes.

This stumped him. With the shoes so buttoned he went to school, but . . . and here is the significant part of the story, he spent the day in careful consideration of the matter.

It happens that this type of sensibility, persisting through forty years, is of extreme, and almost unique, value in a land teeming with clever people, all capable of competent and almost instantaneous extroversion; during the last twenty of these years it has distinguished Dr Williams from the floral and unconscious minds of the populace and from the snappy go-getters who'der seen wot wuz rong in er moment.

It has prevented our author from grabbing ready-made conclusions, and from taking too much for granted.

There are perhaps, or perhaps have been milieux where the reflective and examining habits would not have conferred, unsupported, a distinction. But chez nous, for as long as I can remember if an article appeared in Munsey's or McClure's, expressing a noble passion (civic or other) one could bank (supposing one were exercising editorial or quasi-editorial functions) on seeing the same article served up again in some fifty lyric expressions within, let us say, three or four months.

"Dr Williams' Position." From *The Literary Essays of Ezra Pound* (Norfolk, Connecticut, 1954), pp. 389-98. Originally printed in *The Dial*, LXXXV (November, 1928), 395-404. All rights reserved. Reprinted by permission of the publishers, New Directions Publishing Corporation, New York.

Our national mind hath about it something 'marvellous porous'; an idea or notion dropped into New York harbour emerges in Santa Fé or Galveston, watered, diluted, but still the same idea or notion, pale but not wholly denatured; and the time of transit is very considerably lower, than any 'record' hitherto known. We have the defects of our qualities, and that very alertness which makes the single American diverting or enlivening in an European assembly often undermines his literary capacity.

For fifteen or eighteen years I have cited Williams as sole known American-dwelling author who could be counted on to oppose some sort of barrier to such penetration; the sole catalectic in whose presence some sort of modification would take place.

Williams has written: 'All I do is to try to understand something in its natural colours and shapes'. There could be no better effort underlying any literary process, or used as preparative for literary process; but it appears, it would seem, almost incomprehensible to men dwelling west of the Atlantic: I don't mean that it appears so in theory, America will swallow anything in theory, all abstract statements are perfectly welcome, given a sufficiently plausible turn. But the concrete example of this literary process, whether by Williams or by that still more unreceived and uncomprehended native hickory Mr Joseph Gould, seems an unrelated and inexplicable incident to our populace and to our 'monde—or whatever it is— littéraire'. We have, of course, distinctly American authors, Mr Frost for example, but there is an infinite gulf between Mr Frost on New England customs, and Mr Gould on race prejudice; Mr Frost having simply taken on, without any apparent self-questioning, a definite type and set of ideas and sensibilities, known and established in his ancestral demesne. That is to say he is 'typical New England'. Gould is no less New England, but parts of his writing could have proceeded equally well from a Russian, a German, or an exceptional Frenchman—the difference between regionalism, or regionalist art and art that has its root in a given locality.

Carlos Williams has been determined to stand or sit as an American. Freud would probably say 'because his father was English' (in fact half English, half Danish). His mother, as ethnologists have before noted, was a mixture of French and Spanish; of late years (the last four or five) Dr Williams has laid claim to a somewhat remote Hebrew connexion, possibly a rabbi in Saragossa, at the time of the siege. He claims American birth, but I strongly suspect that he emerged on shipboard just off Bedloe's Island and that his dark and serious eyes gazed up in their first sober contemplation at the Statue and its brazen and monstrous nightshirt.

At any rate he has not in his ancestral endocrines the arid curse of our nation. None of his immediate forebears burnt witches in Salem,[1] or attended assemblies for producing prohibitions. His father was in the rum trade; the rich ichors of the Indes, Hollands, Jamaicas, Goldwasser, Curaoças provided the infant William with material sustenance. Spanish was not a strange tongue, and the trade profited by discrimination, by dissociations performed with the palate. All of which belongs to an American yesterday, and is as gone as les caves de Mouquin.

From this secure ingle William Carlos was able to look out of his circumjacence and see it as something interesting *but exterior;* and he could not by any possibility resemble any member of the Concord School. He was able to observe national phenomena without necessity for constant vigilance over himself, there was no instinctive fear that if he forgot himself he might be like some really unpleasant Ralph Waldo; neither is he, apparently, filled with any vivid desire to murder the indescribable dastards who betray the work of the national founders, who spread the fish-hooks of bureaucracy in our once, perhaps, pleasant bypaths.

One might accuse him of being, blessedly, the observant foreigner, perceiving American vegetation and landscape quite directly, as something put there for him to look at; and his contemplative habit extends, also blessedly, to the fauna.

When Mr Wanamaker's picture gallery burned in the dead of winter I was able to observe the destruction of faked Van Dykes, etc., *comme spectacle,* the muffler'd lads of the village tearing down gold frames in the light of the conflagration, the onyx-topped tables against the blackness were still more 'tableau' and one could think detachedly of the French Revolution. Mr Wanamaker was nothing to me, he paid his employees badly, and I knew the actual spectacle was all I should ever get out of him. I cannot, on the other hand, observe the nation befouled by Volsteads and Bryans, without anger; I cannot see liberties that have lasted for a century thrown away for nothing, for worse than nothing, for slop; frontiers tied up by an imbecile bureaucracy exceeding 'anything known in Russia under the Czars' without indignation.[2]

And by just this susceptibility on my part Williams, as author, has the no small advantage. If he wants to 'do' anything about what he sees, this desire for action does not rise until he has meditated in

---

[1] Note: We didn't burn them, we hanged them. T. S. E. [T. S. Eliot, the editor of *The Literary Essays of Ezra Pound*]

[2] This comparison to Russia is not mine, but comes from a Czarist official who had been stationed in Washington.

full and at leisure. Where I see scoundrels and vandals, he sees a spectacle or an ineluctable process of nature. Where I want to kill at once, he ruminates, and if this rumination leads to anger it is an almost inarticulate anger, that may but lend colour to style, but which stays almost wholly in the realm of his art. I mean it is a qualificative, contemplative, does not drive him to some ultra-artistic or non-artistic activity.

Even recently where one of his characters clearly expresses a dissatisfaction with the American milieu, it is an odium against a condition of mind, not against overt acts or institutions.

II

The lack of celerity in his process, the unfamiliarity with facile or with established solutions would account for the irritation his earlier prose, as I remember it, caused to sophisticated Britons. 'How any man could go on talking about such things!' and so on. But the results of this sobriety of unhurried contemplation, when apparent in such a book as *In the American Grain,* equally account for the immediate appreciation of Williams by the small number of French critics whose culture is sufficiently wide to permit them to read any modern tongue save their own.

Here, at last, was an America treated with a seriousness and by a process comprehensible to an European.

One might say that Williams has but one fixed idea, as an author; i.e., he starts where an European would start if an European were about to write of America: sic: America is a subject of interest, one must inspect it, analyse it, and treat it as subject. There are plenty of people who think they 'ought' to write 'about' America. This is a wholly different kettle of fish. There are also numerous people who think that the given subject has an inherent interest simply because it is American and that this gives it ipso facto a dignity or value above all other possible subjects; Williams may even think he has, or may once have thought he had this angle of attack, but he hasn't.

After a number of years, and apropos of a given incident he has (first quarterly number of *transition*) given a perfectly clear verbal manifestation of his critical attitude. It is that of his most worthy European contemporaries, and of all good critics. It is also symptomatic of New York that his analysis of the so-called criticisms of Antheil's New York concert should appear in Paris, a year after the event, in an amateur periodical.

The main point of his article being that no single one of the

critics had made the least attempt at analysis, or had in any way
tried to tell the reader what the music consisted of, what were its
modes or procedures. And that this was, of course, what the critics
were, or would in any civilised country have been, there for. This
article is perhaps Williams' most important, or at any rate most
apposite, piece of critical writing; failing a wide distribution of the
magazine in which it appeared, it should be reprinted in some more
widely distributable journal.[3]

It would seem that the illusion of 'progress' is limited, chez nous,
to the greater prevalence of erotic adventure, whether developed in
quality or merely increased in quantity I have no present means of
deciding; the illusion as to any corresponding 'progress' or catch-
ing-up in affairs of the intellect, would seem to rise from the fact
that in our literary milieux certain things are now known that were
not known in 1912; but this does not constitute a change of rela-
tion, i.e. does not prove that America is not still fifteen years or
twenty years or more 'behind the times'. We must breed a non-
Mabie, non-Howells type of author. And of the possible types Wil-
liams and Gould serve as our best examples—as distinct from the
porous types.

I mean, not by this sentence, but by the whole trend of this ar-
ticle: when a creative act occurs in America 'no one' seems aware
of what is occurring. In music we have chefs d'orchestre, not com-
posers, and we have something very like it in letters, though the
distinction is less obvious.

Following this metaphor, it is undeniable that part of my time,
for example, has been put into orchestral directing. Very little of
Dr Williams' energy has been so deflected. If he did some Rimbaud
forty years late it was nevertheless composition, and I don't think he
knew it was Rimbaud until after he finished his operation.

Orchestral directing is 'all right' mais c'est pas la même chose. We
are still so generally obsessed by monism and monotheistical back-
wash, and ideas of orthodoxy that we (and the benighted Britons)
can hardly observe a dissociation of ideas without thinking a censure
is somehow therein implied.

We are not, of course we are not, free from the errors of post-
reformation Europe. The triviality of philosophical writers through
the last few centuries is extraordinary, in the extent that is, that
they have not profited by modes of thought quite common to
biological students; in the extent that they rely on wholly un-
founded assumptions, for no more apparent reason than that these

[3] The essay is included in Williams' *Selected Essays*. [ED.]

assumptions are currently and commonly made. Reputed philoso-
phers will proceed (four volumes at a time) as if the only alterna-
tive for monism were dualism; among distinguished literati, si licet,
taking personal examples: Mr Joyce will argue for hours as if one's
attack on Christianity were an attack on the Roman church *in
favour of* Luther or Calvin or some other half-baked ignoramus and
the 'protestant' conventicle. Mr Eliot will reply, even in print, to
Mr Babbitt as if some form of Christianity or monotheism were
the sole alternative to irreligion; and as if monism or monotheism
were anything more than an hypothesis agreeable to certain types
of very lazy mind too weak to bear an uncertainty or to remain in
'uncertainty'.

And, again, for such reasons William Williams, and may we say,
his Mediterranean equipment, have an importance in relation to
his temporal intellectual circumjacence.

Very well, he does not 'conclude'; his work has been 'often form-
less', 'incoherent', opaque, obscure, obfuscated, confused, truncated,
etc.

I am not going to say: 'form' is a non-literary component shoved
on to literature by Aristotle or by some non-litteratus who told
Aristotle about it. Major form is not a non-literary component. But
it can do us no harm to stop an hour or so and consider the number
of very important chunks of world-literature in which form, major
form, is remarkable mainly for absence.

There is a corking plot to the *Iliad,* but it is not told us in the
poem or at least not in the parts of the poem known to history as
The Iliad. It would be hard to find a worse justification of the
theories of dramatic construction than the *Prometheus* of Aeschylus.
It will take a brighter lad than the author of these presents to
demonstrate the element of form in Montaigne or in Rabelais;
Lope has it, but it is not the 'Aristotelian' beginning, middle and
end, it is the quite reprehensible: BEGINNING WHOOP and
then any sort of a trail off. *Bouvard and Pécuchet* wasn't even fin-
ished by its author. And of all these Lope is the only one we could
sacrifice without inestimable loss and impoverishment.

The component of these great works and *the* indispensable com-
ponent is texture; which Dr Williams indubitably has in the best,
and in increasingly frequent, passages of his writing.

III

In current American fiction that has, often, quite a good deal of
merit, and which has apparently been concocted with effort and

goodish intentions, the failure to attain first-rateness seems to be mainly of two sorts: The post-Zolas or post-realists deal with subject matter, human types, etc., so simple that one is more entertained by Fabre's insects or Hudson's birds and wild animals. The habits or the reactions of 'an ant' or 'a chaffinch' emerge in a more satisfactory purity or at least in some modus that at least seems to present a more firm and sustaining pabulum to reflection.

Secondly: there are the perfumed writers. They aim, one believes, at olde lavender; but the ultimate aroma lacks freshness. 'Stale meringue', 'last week's custard' and other metaphorical expressions leap to mind when one attempts to give an impression of their quality. One 'ought' perhaps to make a closer analysis and give the receipt for the fadeur; though like all mediocre dilutations it is harder to analyse than the clearer and fresher substance. When I was fourteen, people used to read novels of the same sort, let us say *The House of a Thousand Candles,* etc., of which one may remember a title, but never remembers anything else, and of which the author's name has, at the end of five or ten years, escaped one.

It is perfectly natural that people wholly surrounded by roughnecks, whether in mid-nineteenth century or in The Hesperian present, should want to indicate the desirability of sweetness and refinement, but . . . these things belong to a different order of existence, different that is from pity, terror, τὸ καλόν, and those things with which art, plastic or that of the writer, is concerned.

Now in reading Williams, let us say this last book *A Voyage to Pagany* or almost anything else he has written, one may often feel: he is wrong. I didn't mean wrong in idea, but: that is the wrong way to write it. He oughtn't to have said that. But there is a residue of effect. The work is always distinct from writing that one finds merely hopeless and in strict sense irremediable.

There is a difference in kind between it and the mass of current writing, about which there is just nothing to be done, and which no series of re-touches, or cuttings away, would clarify, or leave hard.

Art very possibly *ought* to be the supreme achievement, the 'accomplished'; but there is the other satisfactory effect, that of a man hurling himself at an indomitable chaos, and yanking and hauling as much of it as possible into some sort of order (or beauty), aware of it both as chaos and as potential.

Form is, indeed, very tiresome when in reading current novels, we observe the thinning residue of pages, 50, 30, and realize that there is now only time (space) for the hero to die a violent death, no other solution being feasible in that number of pages.

To come at it another way: There are books that are clever enough, good enough, well enough done to fool the people who don't know, or to divert one in hours of fatigue. There are other books—and they may be often less clever, and may often show less accomplishment—which, despite their ineptitudes, and lack of accomplishment, or 'form', and finish, contain something for the best minds of the time, a time, any time. If *Pagany* is not Williams' best book, if even on some counts, being his first long work, it is his worst, it indubitably contains pages and passages that are worth any one's while, and that provide mental cud for any ruminant tooth.

<h2 style="text-align:center">IV</h2>

And finally, to comply with those requirements for critics which Dr Williams has outlined in his censure of Mr Antheil's critics: The particular book that is occasion for this general discussion of Williams, *A Voyage to Pagany*,[4] has not very much to do with the 'art of novel writing', which Dr Williams has fairly clearly abjured. Its plot-device is the primitive one of 'a journey', frankly avowed. Entire pages could have found place in a simple autobiography of travel.

In the genealogy of writing it stems from *Ulysses*, or rather we would say better: Williams' *The Great American Novel*, 80 pages, Three Mountains Press, 1923, was Williams' first and strongest derivation from *Ulysses*, an 'inner monologue', stronger and more gnarled, or stronger *because* more gnarled at least as I see it, than the *Pagany*.

The other offspring from *Ulysses*, the only other I have seen possessing any value, is John Rodker's *Adolphe*, 1920. The two books are greatly different. *The Great American Novel* is simply the application of Joycean method to the American circumjacence. The *Adolphe*, professedly taking its schema from Benjamin Constant, brings the Joycean methodic inventions into a form; slighter than *Ulysses*, as a rondeau is slighter than a canzone, but indubitably a 'development', a definite step in general progress of writing; having, as have at least two other novels by Rodker, its definite shaped construction. And yet, if one read it often enough, the element of form emerges in *The Great American Novel*, not probably governing the whole, but in the shaping of at least some of the chapters, notably Chapter VII, the one beginning 'Nuevo Mundo'.

---

[4] *A Voyage to Pagany*, by William Carlos Williams (New York: The Macaulay Company, 1928), 338 pp.

As to subject or problem, the *Pagany* relates to the Jamesian
problem of U.S.A. *v.* Europe, the international relation, etc.; the
particular equation of the Vienna milieu has had recent treatment
'from the other end on' in Joseph Bard's *Shipwreck in Europe,*
more sprightly and probably less deeply concerned with the salva-
tion of the protagonist; I think the continental author mentions as
a general and known post-war quantity: the American or Ameri-
cans who comes or come to Vienna to find out why they can't enjoy
life, even after getting a great deal of money.

In the American Grain remains, I imagine, Dr Williams' book
having the greater interest for the European reader. In the looseish
structure of the *Pagany* I don't quite make out what, unless it be
simple vagary of the printer, has caused the omission of 'The Venus'
(July *Dial*), pages obviously written to occur somewhere in the
longer work, though they do form a whole in themselves, and pose
quite clearly the general question, or at least one phase of the ques-
tion in the *Pagany*.

In all the books cited,[5] the best pages of Williams—at least for
the present reviewer—are those where he has made the least effort
to fit anything into either story, book, or (in *In the American Grain*)
into an essay. I would almost move from that isolated instance to
the generalization that plot, major form, or outline should be left
to authors who feel some inner need for the same; even let us say a
very strong, unusual, unescapable need for these things; and to
books where the said form, plot, etc., springs naturally from the
matter treated. When put on ab exteriore, they probably lead only
to dullness, confusion or remplissage or the 'falling between two
stools'. I don't mean that Williams 'falls'; he certainly has never
loaded on enough shapings to bother one. As to his two dialectical
ladies? Of course he may know ladies who argue like that. There
may be ladies who so argue, aided by Bacchus. In any case the effect
of one human on another is such that Williams may elicit such
dialectic from ladies who in presence of a more dialectic or voluble
male would be themselves notably less so. No one else now writing
would have given us the sharp clarity of the medical chapters.

As to the general value of Carlos Williams' poetry I have nothing
to retract from the affirmation of its value that I made ten years ago,
nor do I see any particular need of repeating that estimate; I should

[5] *The Tempers* (London: Elkin Mathews, 1913); *Al Que Quiere* (Boston: The
Four Seas Company, 1917); *Kora in Hell* (Boston: The Four Seas Company,
1920); *Sour Grapes* (Boston: The Four Seas Company, 1921); *The Great American
Novel* (Paris: Three Mountains Press, 1923); *In the American Grain* (New York:
Albert and Charles Boni, 1925); *A Voyage to Pagany* (1928).

have to say the same things, and it would be with but a pretence or camouflage of novelty.

When an author preserves, by any means whatsoever, his integrity, I take it we ought to be thankful. We retain a liberty to speculate as to how he might have done better, what paths would conduce to, say, progress in his next opus, etc., to ask whether for example Williams would have done better to have read W. H. Hudson than to have been interested in Joyce. At least there is place for reflection as to whether the method of Hudson's *A Traveller in Little Things* would serve for an author so concerned with his own insides as is Williams; or whether Williams himself isn't at his best —retaining interest in the uncommunicable or the hidden roots of the consciousness of people he meets, but confining his statement to presentation of their objective manifests.

No one but a fantastic impressionist or a fanatic subjectivist or introversionist will try to answer such a question save in relation to a given specific work.

Three Essays on Williams

by Marianne Moore

I. Kora in Hell, by William Carlos Williams*

"The unready would deny tough cords to the wind because they cannot split a storm endwise and wrap it upon spools."

This statement exemplifies a part of what gives to the work of William Carlos Williams, "a character by itself." It is a concise, energetic disgust, a kind of intellectual hauteur which one usually associates with the French.

The acknowledgement of our debt to the imagination, constitutes, perhaps, his positive value. Compression, colour, speed, accuracy and that restraint of instinctive craftsmanship which precludes anything dowdy or laboured—it is essentially these qualities that we have in his work. Burke speaks of the imagination as the most intensive province of pleasure and pain and defines it as a creative power of the mind, representing at pleasure the images of things in the order and manner in which they were received by the senses or in combining them in a new manner and according to a different order. Dr. Williams in his power over the actual, corroborates this statement. Observe how, by means of his rehabilitating power of the mind, he is able to fix the atmosphere of a moment:

"It is still warm enough to slip from the woods into the lake's edge . . . and snake's eggs lie curling in the sun on the lonely summit."

* "Kora in Hell, by William Carlos Williams" by Marianne Moore. From Contact, No. 4 (Summer 1921), pp. 5-8. Reprinted by permission of Marianne Moore and Mrs. Florence H. Williams. I have made a few silent corrections of obvious typographical errors in the original. Quotations from Kora in Hell in this review are reprinted by permission of Lawrence Ferlinghetti and City Lights Books. Some of the quotations are from the Prologue to Kora in Hell. This is not reprinted in the City Lights edition of Kora, but is included in Williams' Selected Essays. I wish to thank Mr. Edward Peters for his kindness and skill in providing me with a transcription of this essay from the copy in the Beinecke Library at Yale.

"Calvary Church with its snail's horns up sniffing the dawn—
o' the wrong side!"

"Always one leaf at the peak twig swirling, swirling and apples
rotting in the ditch."

"By the brokenness of his composition," he writes, "the poet
makes himself master of a certain weapon which he could possess
himself of in no other way." We do not so much feel the force of
this statement as we feel that there is in life, as there is in Sir
Francis Bacon—in the ability to see resemblances in things which
are dissimilar; in the ability to see such differences, a special kind
of imagination is required, which Dr. Williams has. Despite his
passion for being himself and his determination not to be at the
mercy of "schoolmasters," it is only one who is academically
sophisticated who could write:

"Fatigued as you are, watch how the mirror sieves out the ex-
traneous," and:

"Of what other thing is greatness composed than a power to
annihilate half truths for a thousandth part of accurate under-
standing."

"Often," he says, "a poem will have merit because of some one
line or even one meritorious word. So it hangs heavily on its
stem but still secure, the tree unwilling to release it."

Such an observation certainly is not the result of pure intuition
or of any informally, semi-consciously exercised mental energy.
It is not, after all, the naive but the authentic upon which he
places value. To the bona fide artist, affectation is degradation
and in his effort to "annihilate half truths," Dr. Williams is hard,
discerning, implacable and deft. If he rates audacity too high as
an aesthetic asset, there can be no doubt that he has courage of
the kind which is a necessity and not merely an admired accessory.
Discerning the world's hardness, his reply is the reply of Carl
Sandburg's boll weevil to threats of sand, hot ashes and the river:
"That'll be ma HOME! That'll be ma HOME!"

"Where does this downhill turn up again?" he says:

"Driven to the wall you'd put claws to your toes and make a
ladder of smooth bricks."

Though restive under advice, he is resigned under the imper-
sonal, inevitable attrition of life.

"One need not be hopelessly cast down," he says, "because he
cannot cut onyx into a ring to fit a lady's finger. . . . There is
neither onyx nor porphyry on these roads—only brown dirt. For
all that, one may see his face in a flower along it—even in this

light. . . . Walk in the curled mudcrusts to one side, hands hang-
ing. Ah well."

To discuss one's friends in print may or may not be necessitated
by fealty to art but whether there is beauty or not in Dr. Williams'
discussion of persons as there is in his discussion of life—in citing
the idiosyncrasies of friends, note his calmness:

"B. pretends to hate most people, . . . but that he really goes
to this trouble I cannot imagine."

Additional marks of health are to be found in his use of idiom.
He says:

"If a woman laughs a little loudly one always thinks that way
of her."

"Throw two shoes on the floor and see how they'll lie if you
think it's all one way."

The sharpened faculties which require exactness, instant satis-
faction and an underpinning of truth are too abrupt in their
activities sometimes to follow; but the niceness and effect of
vigour for which they are responsible are never absent from Dr.
Williams' work and its crisp exterior is one of its great distinctions.
He again reminds one of the French. John Burroughs says of French
drivers of drays and carts, "They are not content with a plain
matter-of-fact whip as an English or American labourer would be,
but it must be a finely modeled stalk, with a long tapering lash,
tipped with the best silk snapper."

"It is silly to go into a 'puckersnatch,' " Dr. Williams says, "be-
cause some brass-button-minded nincompoop in Kensington flies
off the handle and speaks openly about our United States prize
poems."

In the following passage, the words "black and peculiar" would
seem to be the snapper:

"A mother will love her children most grotesquely. . . . She will
be most willing toward that daughter who thwarts her most and
not toward the little kitchen helper. So where one is mother to
any great number of people she will love best perhaps some child
whose black and peculiar hair is an exact replica of that of the
figure in Velásquez' Infanta Maria Theresa or some Italian matron
whose largeness of manner takes in the whole street."

Despite Dr. Williams' championing of the school of ignorance,
or rather of no school but experience, there is in his work the
authoritativeness, the wise silence which knows schools and fashions
well enough to know that completeness is further down than
professional intellectuality and modishness can go.

"Lamps carry far, believe me," he says, "in lieu of sunshine."

"What can it mean to you that a child wears pretty clothes and speaks three languages or that its mother goes to the best shops? . . . Men . . . buy finery and indulge in extravagant moods in order to piece out their lack with other matter."

"Kindly stupid hands, kindly coarse voices, . . . infinitely detached, infinitely beside the question . . . and night is done and the green edge of yesterday has said all it could."

"In middle life the mind passes to a variegated October. This is the time youth in its faulty aspirations has set for the achievement of great summits. But having attained the mountain top one is not snatched into a cloud but the descent proffers its blandishments quite as a matter of course. At this the fellow is cast into a great confusion and rather plaintively looks about to see if any has fared better than he."

Dr. Williams' wisdom, however, is not absolute and he is sometimes petulant.

"Nowadays poets spit upon rhyme and rhetoric," he says. His work provides examples of every rhetorical principle insisted on by rhetoricians and one wonders upon what ground he has been able to persuade himself that poets spit upon rhyme? Possibly by rhetoric, he means balderdash; in this case then, we are merely the poorer by one, of proofs for his accuracy.

"It is folly," he says, "to accept remorse as a criticism of conduct."

One's manners, good or bad, are conventionalized instincts and conduct as a combination of manners and volition, predicates whatever is the result of it, so that remorse is automatically a criticism of conduct; but Dr. Williams is essentially a poet. It is true, as he says, that "by direct onslaught or by some back road of the intention the gifted will win the recognition of the world." His book is alive with meaning; in it, "thoughts are trees" and "leaves load the branches." But one who sets out to appraise him has temerity, since he speaks derisively of the wish of certain of his best friends to improve his work and, after all, the conflict between the tendency to aesthetic anarchy and the necessity for self-imposed discipline must take care of itself.

As for leaving nothing unsaid—or to be accurate, something unsaid—there is no topic which a thoughtful person would refuse to discuss if gain were to result; but so far as one can see, the peculiar force of Dr. Williams' work does not gain by an allusion to topics of which the average person never thinks unless inescapably for humanitarian reasons. Dr. Williams is too sincere to wish to be fashionable and that one so rich in imagination should have to be thrifty in the use of poetic material is preposterous. One's perspicacity here meets a stone wall.

So disdainful, so complex a poet as Dr. Williams, receives at best half treatment from the average critic or from the ambitious critic, such untruthful, half specific approbation as, "Ah, quite deep; I see to the bottom." This is to be expected. There is in Dr. Williams an appetite for the essential and in how many people may one find it? How many poets, old or new, have written anything like "January Morning" in *Al Que Quiere!*, like the second paragraph of Improvisation XVII in the present volume, and pre-eminently, the "Portrait of the Author" in a recent number of *Contact*? Withholding comment upon the title, this poem is a super-achievement. It preserves the atmosphere of a moment, into which the impertinence of life cannot intrude. In the sense conveyed, of remoteness from what is detestable, in the effect of balanced strength, in the flavour of newness in presentation, it is unique.

II. *A Poet of the Quattrocento**

It was Ezra Pound's conviction some years ago, that there could be "an age of awakening in America" which would "overshadow the quattrocento." Hopeful for us at that time, "our opportunity is greater than Leonardo's," said Mr Pound; "we have more aliment," and never really neglectful of us, he has commended in us, "Mr Williams' praiseworthy opacity." "There is distinctness and color," he observed, "as was shown in his 'Postlude,' in 'Des Imagistes'; but there is beyond these qualities the absolute conviction of a man with his feet on the soil, on a soil personally and peculiarly his own. He is rooted. He is at times almost inarticulate, but he is never dry, never without sap in abundance."

This metaphor of the tree seems highly appropriate to William Carlos Williams—who writes of seedling sycamores, of walnuts and willows—who several years ago, himself seemed to W. C. Blum "by all odds the hardiest specimen in these parts." [1] In his modestly emphatic respect for America he corroborates Henry James's conviction that young people should "stick fast and sink up to their necks in everything their own countries and climates can give,"

* "A Poet of the Quattrocento" by Marianne Moore. From *The Dial*, LXXXII (1927), 213-15. Copyright © 1927 by The Dial Publishing Company. Reprinted by permission of Marianne Moore and *The Dial* magazine.
[1] Cf. American Letter by W. C. Blum, *The Dial*, LXX (January–June, 1921), 562-68.

and his feeling for the *place* lends poetic authority to an illusion
of ours, that sustenance may be found here, which is adapted to
artists. Imagination can profit by a journey, acquainting itself with
everything pertaining to its wish that it can gather from European
sources, Doctor Williams says. But it is apparent to him that
"American plumbing, American bridges, indexing systems, loco-
motives, printing presses, city buildings, farm implements and a
thousand other things" are liked and used, and it is not folly to
hope that the very purest works of the imagination may also be
found among us. Doctor Williams is in favour of escape from
"strained associations," from "shallowness," from such substitutes
as "congoleum—building paper with a coating of enamel." The
staying at home principle could not, he is sure, be a false one
where there is vigorous living force with buoyancy of imagination
—as there was apparently in Shakespeare—the artist's excursion
being into "perfection" and "technical excellence"! "Such names
as Homer, the blind; Scheherazade, who lived under threat—Their
compositions have as their excellence, an identity with life since
they are as actual, as sappy as the leaf of the tree which never
moves from one spot." He has visited various places and studied
various writings and a traveller can as Bacon says, "prick in some
flowers of that he hath learned abroad." In the main, however,
Doctor Williams' topics are American—crowds at the movies

> with the closeness and
> universality of sand,

turkey nests, mushrooms among the fir trees, mist rising from the
duck pond, the ball game:

> It is summer, it is the solstice
> the crowd is
>
> cheering, the crowd is laughing

or

"It is spring. Sunshine . . . dumped among factories . . . down
a red dirt path to four goats. . . . I approach the smallest goat
timidly. . . . It draws away beginning to wind its tie rope around
the tree. . . . I back the creature around the tree till it can go no
further, the cord all wound up. Gingerly I take it by the ear. It
tries to crowd between me and the tree." I drive it "around the
tree again until the rope is entirely unwound. The beast immedi-
ately finds new violent green tufts of grass in some black mud

half under some old dried water-soaked weedstalks. . . . To the right of the path the other goat comes forward boldly but stops short and sniffs, . . . It ventures closer. Gna-ha-ha-ha-ha! (as in a hat). Very softly. The small goat answers."

> O spring days, swift
> and mutable, wind blowing
> four ways, hot and cold.

Essentially not a "repeater of things second-hand," Doctor Williams is in his manner of contemplating with new eyes, old things, shabby things, and other things, a poet, Metre he thinks of as an "essential of the work, one of its words." That which is to some imperceptible, is to him the "milligram of radium" that he values. He is rightly imaginative in not attempting to decide; or rather, in deciding not to attempt to say how wrong these readers are, who find his poems unbeautiful or "positively repellant." As he had previously asked, "Where does this downhill turn up again? Driven to the wall you'd put claws to your toes and make a ladder of smooth bricks."

Facts presented to us by him in his prose account of The Destruction of Tenochtitlan, could not be said to be "new," but the experience ever, in encountering that which has been imaginatively assembled, is exceedingly new. One recalls in reading these pages, the sense augmented, of "everything which the world affords," of "the drive upward, toward the sun and the stars"; and foremost as poetry, we have in a bewilderingly great, neatly ordered pageant of magnificence, Montezuma, "this American cacique," "so delicate," "so full of tinkling sounds and rhythms, so tireless of invention."

One sees nothing terrifying in what Doctor Williams calls a "modern traditionalism," but to say so is to quibble. Incuriousness, emptiness, a sleep of the faculties, are an end of beauty; and Doctor Williams is vivid. Perhaps he is modern. He addresses himself to the imagination. He is "keen" and "compact." "At the ship's prow" as he says the poet should be, he is glad to have his "imaginary" fellow-creatures with him. Unless we are very literal, this should be enough.

III. *"Things Others Never Notice"* *

Struggle, like the compression which propels the steam-engine, is a main force in William Carlos Williams. He "looks a bit like that grand old plaster cast, Lessing's Laocoön," Wallace Stevens says in the introduction to this book. And the breathless budding of thought from thought is one of the results and charms of the pressure configured. With an abandon born of inner security, Dr. Williams somewhere nicknames the chain of incontrovertibly logical apparent non-sequiturs, rigmarole; and a consciousness of life and intrepidity is characteristically present in "Stop: Go"—

> a green truck
> dragging a concrete mixer
> passes
> in the street—
> the clatter and true sound
> of verse—

Disliking the tawdriness of unnecessary explanation, the detracting compulsory connective, stock speech of any kind, he sets the words down, "each note secure in its own posture—singularly woven." "The senseless unarrangement of wild things" which he imitates makes some kinds of correct writing look rather foolish; and as illustrating that combination of energy and composure which is the expertness of the artist, he has never drawn a clearer self-portrait than "Birds and Flowers," part 2:

> What have I done
> to drive you away? It is
> winter, true enough, but
>
> this day I love you.
> This day
> there is no time at all
>
> more than in under
> my ribs where anatomists
> say the heart is—

---

* "Things Others Never Notice" by Marianne Moore. From *Poetry*, XLIV (1934), 103-6. Copyright © 1934 by Harriet Monroe. Reprinted by permission of Marianne Moore and *Poetry*. This was written as a review of *Collected Poems 1921-1931*, by William Carlos Williams, with Preface by Wallace Stevens (New York: The Objectivist Press, 1934).

> And just today you
> will not have me. Well,
> to-morrow it may be snowing—
>
> I'll keep after you. Your
> repulse of me is no more
> than a rebuff to the weather—
>
> If we make a desert of
> ourselves—we make
> a desert . . .

William Carlos Williams objects to urbanity—to sleek and natty effects—and this is a good sign if not always a good thing. Yet usually nothing could better the dashing shrewdness of the pattern as he develops it and cuts it off at the acutely right point.

With the bee's sense of polarity he searches for a flower and that flower is representation. Likenesses here are not reminders of the object, they are likenesses:

> And there's the river with thin ice upon it
> fanning out half over the black
> water, the free middlewater racing under its
> ripples that move crosswise on the stream.

He is drugged with romance—"O unlit candle with the soft white plume"—but like the bee, is neither a waif nor a fool. Argus-eyed, energetic, insatiate, compassionate, undeceived, he says in "Immortal" (in *The Tempers*), "Yes, there is one thing braver than all flowers, . . . And thy name, lovely One, is Ignorance." Wide-eyed resignation of this kind helps some to be cynical but it makes Dr. Williams considerate; sorry for the tethered bull, the circus sea-elephant, for the organ-grinder "sourfaced," for the dead man "needing a shave—"

> the dog won't have to
> sleep on his potatoes
> any more to keep them
> from freezing—

He ponders "the justice of poverty its shame its dirt" and pities the artist's prohibited energy as it patiently does for the common weal what it ought to do, and the poem read by critics who have no inkling of what it's about. But the pathos is incidental. The "ability to be drunk with a sudden realization of value in things others never notice" can metamorphose our detestable reasonableness and offset a whole planetary system of deadness. "The burning liquor of the moonlight" makes provable things mild by comparison. Art, that is to say, has its effect on the artist and also on the patron; and in Dr. Williams we have an example of art that disregards crochets and specifications. The poem often is about nothing that we wish to give our attention to, but if it is something he wishes our attention for, what is urgent for him becomes urgent for us. His uncompromising conscientiousness sometimes seems misplaced; he is at times almost insultingly unevasive, but there is in him—and this must be our consolation—that dissatisfied expanding energy, the emotion, the cock-spur of the medieval dialectician, the "therefore" that is the distinguishing mark of the artist.

Various poems that are not here, again suggest the bee—the plausibility of keeping bees and preëmpting the disposition of the honey.

Dr. Williams does not compromise, and Wallace Stevens is another resister whose way of saying is as important as what is said. Mr. Stevens' presentation of the book refreshes a grievance—the scarcity of prose about verse from one of the few persons who should have something to say. But poetry in America has not died, so long as these two "young sycamores" are able to stand the winters that we have, and the inhabitants.

William Carlos Williams: Two Judgments

by Kenneth Burke

I. Heaven's First Law*

It had once been my privilege to see a page written by William Carlos Williams on which he undertook to reproduce nine times the lovely sunshine thought, "Order is Heaven's first law." Now, by the fifth time, the poet became noticeably impatient, and from the seventh on the copy was completely unreadable. The ninth version was a mere wavy line, broken in four places. At first I took this to be quite damning; but on second thought, what use could Williams make of order? He thinks in an entirely different set of terms. To add organization to his poetry would have no more meaning than to insist that his lines begin in alphabetical rotation.

What Williams sees, he sees in a flash. And if there is any correlation whatsoever, it is a certain determined joyousness in a poet who would find it awkward to weep. For as his arch-enemy has noted, Williams is a bad Freudian case whose poetry is certainly not allowed to come out the way it came in. But beyond this very reasonable pudency, which he shares with no less an artist than Flaubert, consistency falls away.

No, Williams is the master of the glimpse. A line of his, suddenly leaping up out of the text, will throw the reader into an unexpected intimacy with his subject, like pushing open a door and advancing one's nose into some foreign face. Given a subject, he will attack it with verve, striking where he can break through its defence, and expecting applause whenever a solid, unmistakable jolt has been landed. It would be mere idleness to give his *ars poetica* in more presumptuous terms. The process is simply this: There is the

* "Heaven's First Law" by Kenneth Burke. From *The Dial*, LXXII (1922), 197-200. Copyright © 1922 by The Dial Publishing Company. Reprinted by permission of Kenneth Burke, Marianne Moore, and *The Dial* magazine. This article was written as a review of *Sour Grapes* by William Carlos Williams (Boston: The Four Seas Company, 1921).

eye, and there is the thing upon which that eye alights; while the relationship existing between the two is a poem.

The difficulty here lies in conveying the virtues of such a method. For the method itself is as common as mud. The minute fixating of a mood, an horizon, a contrast; if one finds there any unusual commendation for Williams it is not in the excellence of his poetics, but in the excellence of his results. His first virtue, therefore, lies in the superiority of *his* minute fixations over those of his ten million competitors. He is a distinguished member of a miserable crew.

Honest people who really think highly enough of words to feel unhappy when they are vague will rejoice that Williams' new volume, *Sour Grapes,* is more sober in this respect than the *Improvisations.* For the *Improvisations* were not finally satisfactory. Clear notes were there in abundance, but they were usually preceded and followed by the usual modern data for mental tests. (How beautiful the association of ideas would have been in art if used in one work, by one man, for one page, and for some end other than that of a beautiful association of ideas.) True, by the mere dissatisfaction of their context, such momentary beatitudes of expression received their full share of enthusiasm, but having twenty sentences of chaos to heighten one sentence of cosmos is too much like thanking God for headaches since they enable us to be happy without them.

Sour Grapes, however, skips a generation and takes after the volume, *Al Que Quiere!* And in these two works, it seems to me, Williams is at his best, since here he is not handicapping his remarkable powers of definition, of lucidity. You may wonder, perhaps, just why the poet is going off in some particular direction; but you are always aware just what this direction is. Here also his inveterate lustiness is up to par; for Williams knows Walt Whitman's smile down to the last wrinkle. If there are logs in the grate, he puts a match to them; if it is a warm Easter morning, he throws off his coat. And if, behind it all, there is evidence of a strong tendency towards transgression, towards, let us say, the mountains of Tibet or a negro harem in Madagascar, such things are there as an irritant rather than as a subject. The face value of the poems will always remain the definition of the poet's own gatepost. His peculiar gifts of expression, if nothing else, dictate this simplification. Williams evidently realizes that his emotions are one thing and his art another, and that those who wish to go beyond his minute fixations can find a great deal more implicated in them; but in the meantime, let the minute fixations suffice.

I should say, therefore, that Williams was engaged in discovering the shortest route between object and subject. And whether it is a flamingo befouling its own tail, or the tired ogling at little girls, or trees stark naked in a wind, one must always recognize the unusual propriety of his poetry, the sureness and directness with which he goes at such things. A fact with him finds its justification in the trimness of the wording.

If a man is walking, it is the first principle of philosophy to say that he is *not* walking, the first principle of science to say that he is placing one foot before the other and bringing the hinder one in turn to the fore, the first principle of art to say that the man is *more than* walking, he is *yearning*: then there are times when scientist, philosopher, and poet all discover of a sudden that by heavens! the man is walking and none other. Now, a good deal of this discovery is in Williams' poetry, and, if I understand the word correctly, is contained in his manifesto praising Contact in art. For I take Contact to mean: man without the syllogism, without the parode, without Spinoza's Ethics, man with nothing but the thing and the feeling of that thing. Sitting down in the warmth to write, for instance, Kant might finally figure it out that man simply must have standards of virtue in spite of the bleakness of the phenomenon-noumenon distinction, and that this virtue could be constructed on the foundations of a categorical imperative. But Williams, sitting down in the warmth to write, would never get over his delight that the wind outside was raging ineffectually; and, in his pronounced sense of comfort, he would write:

January

Again I reply to the triple winds
running chromatic fifths of derision
outside my window:
                              Play louder.
You will not succeed. I am
bound more to my sentences
the more you batter at me
to follow you.
                              And the wind,
as before, fingers perfectly
its derisive music

Seen from this angle, Contact might be said to resolve into the counterpart of Culture, and Williams becomes thereby one of our most distinguished Neanderthal men. His poetry deals with the

coercions of nature—and by nature I mean iron rails as well as iron
ore—rather than with the laborious structure of ideas man has
erected above nature. His hatred of the idea in art is consequently
pronounced, and very rightly brings in its train a complete disinter-
est in form. (Note: Form in literature must always have its begin-
nings in idea. In fact, our word for idea comes from a Greek word
whose first meaning is "form.") The Contact writer deals with
his desires; the Culture writer must erect his desires into principles
and deal with those principles rather than with the desires; the *Ur-
phenomen,* in other words, becomes with the man of Culture of less
importance than the delicate and subtle instruments with which he
studies it.

Williams, however, must go back to the source. And the process
undeniably has its beauties. What, for instance, could be more
lost, more uncorrelated, a closer Contact, a greater triumph of anti-
Culture, than this poem:

The Great Figure

Among the rain
and lights
I saw the figure 5
in gold
on a red
firetruck
moving
with weight and urgency
tense
unheeded
to gong clangs
siren howls
and wheels rumbling
through the dark city.

II. *William Carlos Williams, 1883-1963*

William Carlos Williams, poet and physician. Trained to crises
of sickness and parturition that often came at odd hours. An ebul-
lient man, sorely vexed in his last years, and now at rest. But he

* "William Carlos Williams, 1883-1963" by Kenneth Burke. Reprinted from
The New York Review of Books, I, 2 (1963), 45-47. Copyright © 1963 by The
New York Review, Inc. Reprinted by permission of *The New York Review of
Books.*

had this exceptional good luck: that his appeal as a person survives in his work. To read his books is to find him warmly there, everywhere you turn.

In some respects, the physician and the poet might be viewed as opposites, as they certainly were at least in the sense that time spent on his patients was necessarily time denied to the writing of poetry. But that's a superficial view. In essence, this man was an imaginative physician and a nosological poet. His great humaneness was equally present in both roles, which contributed essentially to the development of each other.

"There is no thing that with a twist of the imagination cannot be something else," he said in an early work, whereby he could both use flowers as an image of lovely womanhood and speak of pathology as a "flower garden." The principle made for great mobility, for constant transformations that might affect a writer in late years somewhat like trying to run a hundred yards in ten seconds flat. At the same time, such shiftiness in the new country of the poet's mind allowed for imaginal deflections that could be at once secretive and expressive. Also (except that the simile fails to bring out the strongly personal aspect of the work) his "objectivism" was like inquiring into baseball not in terms of the rule book, but rather by noting the motions and designs which the players in some one particular game might make with reference to the trajectories of a sphere that, sometimes thrown, sometimes struck, took various courses across a demarcated field. Such constant attempts to see things afresh, as "facts," gave him plenty to do. For he proceeded circumstantially, without intellectualistic shortcuts—and with the combined conscientiousness of both disciplines, as man of medicine and medicine man.

An anecdote might help indicate what I have in mind about Williams. (For present purposes, I think, we should refer to him thus, though the usage does greatly misrepresent my personal attitude.) Some years after Williams had retired from his practice as a physician, and ailments had begun to cripple him, we were walking slowly on a beach in Florida. A neighbor's dog decided to accompany us, but was limping. I leaned down, aimlessly hoping to help the dog (which became suddenly frightened, and nearly bit me). Then Williams took the paw in his left hand (the right was now less agile) and started probing for the source of the trouble. It was a gesture at once expert and imaginative, something in which to have perfect confidence, as both the cur and I saw in a flash. Feeling between the toes lightly, quickly, and above all *surely*, he spotted a burr, removed it without the slightest cringe on the dog's part—and the three of us were again on our way along the beach.

I thought to myself (though not then clearly enough to say so): "And here I've learned one more thing about Williams' doctrine of 'contact.'" It concerned the *"tactus eruditus,"* and I quote words that he had tossed, as a line all by itself, into a somewhat rough-and-tumble outburst, "This is My Platform," he had written in the twenties.

Some forty years earlier, when I had first haggled with him about this slogan (which is as basic to an understanding of him as the statement of poetic policy he makes several times in his writings, "No ideas but in things"), the talk of "contact" had seemed most of all to imply that an interest in local writing and language should replace my absorption in Thomas Mann's German and André Gide's French. Next, it suggested a cult of "Amurricanism" just at the time when many young writers, copying Pound and Eliot, were on the way to self-exile in Europe while more were soon to follow. (I mistakenly thought that I was to be one of them.) Further, it seemed to imply the problematical proposition that one should live in a small town like Rutherford rather than in the very heart of Babylon (or in some area that, if not central to the grass roots of the nation, was at least close to the ragweed).

But over the years, as Williams persisted unstoppably in his ways, the nature of his writings gradually made it clear that the implications of "contact" and its particular kind of "anti-poetry" were quite different, and went much deeper. I feel sure that, whatever may be our uncertainties about the accidents of his doctrine, its essence resides in the kind of physicality imposed upon his poetry by the nature of his work as a physician. Thus, as with the incident of the dog, my understanding of his slogan took a notable step forward when, some time after giving up his practice, he said explosively that he missed the opportunity to get his hands on things (and he made gestures to do with the delivering of a child). However, my thesis is not made any easier by the fact that, while including Aaron Burr among his band because Burr felt the need "to touch, to hear, to see, to smell, to taste" (thus being "intact" in the ways of contact), at the same time Williams disapproved of Franklin, "the face on the penny stamp," and complained with regard to Franklin's perpetual tinkering: "To want to touch, not to wish anything to remain clean, aloof—comes always of a kind of timidity, from fear."

The point is this: For Williams any natural or poetic concern with the body as a sexual object was reinforced and notably modified by a professional concern with the body as a suffering or diseased object. (Think how many of his stories testify to his sympathetic yet picturesquely entertaining encounters with wide areas of both physical and social morbidity.) The same relation to the human animal in terms of bodily disabilities led him to a kind of democracy quite unlike Whitman's, despite the obvious influence of Whitman upon him. "After some years of varied experience with the bodies of the rich and the poor a man finds little to distinguish between them, bulks them as one and bases his working judgments on other matters." (In any case, the political editorializing in Whitman's come-one-come-all attitude had lost its meaning, other than as a pleasant sentiment, in proportion as Congress erected legal barriers to the flow of immigrants by a quota system.)

The same stress upon the all-importance of the bodily element accounts also for the many cruel references to subsidence that are scattered through *The Collected Later Poems*. (We shall later get to the earlier, more athletic stages.) Consider "The Night Rider," for instance, that begins, "scoured like a conch/or the moon's shell/I ride from my love/through the damp night," and ends: "the pulse a remembered pulse/of full-tide gone." The theme naturally lends itself to other kinds of imagery: "The old horse dies slow"; the portrait of an old goat, "listless in its assured sanctity"; a time of drought ("The Words Lying Idle"); the tree, stretched on the garage roof, after a hurricane; homage to the woodpecker, "stabbing there with a barbed tongue which *succeeds*"; apostrophizing the self, "why do you try/so hard to be a man? You are/a lover! Why adopt/the reprehensible absurdities of/an inferior attitude?"; with the mind like a tidal river, "the tide will/change/and rise again, maybe"; there is the theme of "The Thoughtful Lover" who finds that "today/the particulars/of poetry" require his "whole attention"; and of a "Bare Tree" he writes, "chop it down/and use the wood/against this biting cold." In this group, certainly, would belong "The Injury," an account of the poet lying in a hospital bed; he hears "an engine/breathing—somewhere/in the night:/— soft coal, soft coal,/soft coal"; in terms of the laboring engine's sounds as he interprets them, he makes plans for the next phase, "the slow way . . . if you can find any way." This expression of dispiritedness wells up so simply, so spontaneously, it is itself a poignantly beautiful instance of spirit. And for a happy and charming variation on such themes, there is "Spring is Here Again, Sir," ending:

> We lay, Floss and I, on
> the grass together, in
> the warm air: a bird flew

into a bush, dipped our
hands in the running water—
cold, too cold; but found
it, to our satisfaction,
as in the past, still wet.

The sullen reference (already quoted) to using the "bare tree" as firewood reminds us that whereas in an early poem fires came "out of the bodies/Of all men that walk with lust at heart," in later poems the theme of fire could be modified by merging with connotations of the purgative. Thus, there is the ecstatic section to do with fire in *Paterson*. And his rightly well-known piece, "Burning the Christmas Greens," interweaves this elation of the purgative with the color that is always the best of omens in Williams' work. I have at times got courage from the thought that a poem of his, entitled "At Kenneth Burke's Place," has for its ending a reference to a greening apple, "smudged with/a sooty life that clings, also,/ with the skin," and despite a bit of rot "still good/even unusual compared with the usual."

But this moves us to a further step in his benignly nosological approach to the subject-matter of poetry. I refer to his interest in the sheer survival of things, so that he would record the quality of an ungainly apple from a gnarled old unpruned, unsprayed tree, "as if a taste long lost and regretted/had in the end, finally, been brought to life again." Thus it seems almost inevitable that he should get around to writing a long poem, "The Desert Music." Along these lines, I have thought that an ideal subject for a poem by him would be a gallant description of weeds, wildflowers, bushes and low trees gradually carving out a livelihood for themselves in the slag piles around Scranton. This would be done without sentimentality. (Poems of his like that can't be sentimental, for they say what's actually there in front of him, as with his lines on the rat, surviving even infections deliberately imposed by the hellish ingenuity of man-made plagues, an animal "well/suited to a world/ conditioned to such human 'tropism/for order' at all cost.") Here would belong his many poems that, by the very accuracy of their description, testify to his delight in scattered, improvised bits of beauty, as with things one can see during that most dismal of transitions, "Approach to a City" (tracks in dirty snow, "snow/pencilled with the stubble of old/weeds," dried flowers in a bar-room window, while "The flags in the heavy/air move against a leaden/ground"). In such observations, he says, he can "refresh" himself. Cannot one easily see how his doctoring figured here, teaching him never to overlook "a mud/livid with decay and life," and where the doctor had found sheer life, challenging the poet to go a step further and spontaneously find it beautiful, as a theologian might have striven to find it good?

See, on this point, "The Hard Core of Beauty," describing things on "the/dead-end highway, abandoned/when the new bridge went in finally." Just stop for a while, go back over that line, ponder on each moment—and I'm sure you'll agree that, whatever its cruel, spare sharpness, there's something softly nostalgic like a voice heard through a mist. Within it there's the thought that never left him, the beauty and cleanness of the river around the falls at Paterson, before its rape by the drastic combination of raw politics, raw technics and raw business. (In earlier years, he referred to the area as "the origin today of the vilest swillhole in christendom, the Passaic river.") All the time the poet-doctor is pointing out, again and again, what survives, there is also the poignancy of what is lost. And in *Paterson,* along with the love, there is the tough, unanswerable, *legalistic documentation* of man's brutal errors, and their costliness to man. As he put it in another book, "Poised against the *Mayflower* is the slave ship." This too was *contact.* And he has done for that damned botched area just west of the Hudson (that hateful traffic-belching squandering of industrial power atop the tidal swamps) something quite incredible: he has made it poignantly songful. He went on singing, singing, singing, while the rivers and the soil and the air and the fires became progressively more polluted in the name of Progress, while more and more of the natural beauties were ripped apart, singing while each year there spread inexorably farther west a cancerous growth of haphazard real-estating that came to enclose his own fine old house in some measure of the general urban sprawl. When the sun rises behind "the moody/water-loving giants of Manhattan," eight miles to the east, they must cast their shadows for a time on the houses west of the Meadows. And in any case the troublous monsters at a distance, magical in the morning or evening mist, did unquestionably cast their shadows on his work.

I have said that Williams was never "sentimental." But I must say more on this point, in view of Wallace Stevens' remark in his preface to Williams' *Collected Poems, 1921-1931:* " 'The Cod Head' is a bit of pure sentimentalization; so is 'The Bull.' " But, as you must expect of Stevens, the word is used in a quite alembicated sense, to name "what vitalizes Williams," and to serve as a proper accompaniment to his "anti-poetic" side. To see most quickly how the two motives work together, one needs but think of a gruffly beautiful line like "the moon is in/the oak tree's crotch." Or "little frogs/with puffed-out throats,/singing in the slime."

I meant that Williams' typical use of imagery does not involve *false* or *forced* sentiment. If I correctly interpret Wallace Stevens' "Nuances of a Theme by Williams" (in *Harmonium*), Stevens meant by sentiment any personal identification with an object, as distinct from an appreciation of it in its pure singularity, without reference to its possible imaginary role as a mirror of mankind.

In this sense, Williams is "sentimental." For all his "objectivist" accuracy, Williams' details are not in essence descriptions of things but portraits of personalities. Typically in his poems the eye (like a laying on of hands), by disguised rituals that are improvised constantly anew, inordinates us into the human nature of things.

As regards the two poems that Stevens specifically mentions, the ending of "The Cod Head" ("a severed cod—/head between two/ green stones—lifting/falling") involves associations that might ultimately fit better with a title somehow combining "severed godhead" and "codpiece"—and something similar is obviously afoot at the end of the poem "The Bull": "milkless/he nods/the hair between his horns/and eyes matted/with hyacinthine curls." As with Marianne Moore, Williams' observations about animals or things are statements about notable traits in people. Along with their ostensible nature, the sympathetic reader gets this deeper dimension as a bonus, an earned increment. Let's be specific. I shall quote a brief item that, if it doesn't seem almost like nonsense, must seem like what it is, a marvel:

> As the cat
> climbed over
> the top of
>
> the jamcloset
> first the right
> forefoot
>
> carefully
> then the hind
> stepped down
>
> into the pit of
> the empty
> flowerpot

Here is the account of a consummate moment in the motions of an unassuming cat, an alleycat, I like to think, that just happened to have a home—plus the inanity of the consummation, as hinted by the empty flowerpot. How differently a dog would have managed, barging in and doubtless bumping the flowerpot over! What trimness the poet brings to his representation of trimness! And in its perfectly comic study of perfection, it is so final, I could easily imagine it being used as the epilogue to something long and arduous. Inevitably, he called the lines just "Poem."

Stevens' point led us away from our main point. But in his own way he leads us back again, when he ends by observing that an alternative preface might have been written presenting Williams as "a kind of Diogenes of contemporary poetry." Diogenes wrote when Greek culture was decidedly in a valetudinarian condition; and though neither poet nor medico, in his proverbial downrightness he could properly be taken to stand for Williams' particular combination of the two.

There are many cases where Williams' diagnostic eye, modified by an urge towards encouragement, becomes the sheerly appreciative eye. Cf. Stevens: "He writes of flowers exquisitely." But it's also a fact, for instance, that whenever Williams bears down on the description of a flower, connotations of love and lovely woman are there implicitly, and quite often explicitly. Thus, in *Stevens'* sense, the poems are inherently "sentimentalized." Whatever the gestures of *haecceitas* (the sense of an object in its sheer thisness), with Williams lyric utterance is essentially a flash of drama, a fragment of narrative, a bit of personal history mirrored as well in talk of a thing as in talk of a person.

And for this reason, given his initial medical slant, the tendency always is towards a matter of welfare. Dante said that the proper subjects for poetry are *venus, virtus* and *salus*. The "anti-poetic" strain in Williams' poetry gives us a medical variant of *salus*, nowhere more startlingly contrived than in this neat abruptness:

To

a child (a boy) bouncing
a ball (a blue ball)—

He bounces it (a toy racket
in his hand) and runs

and catches it (with his
left hand) six floors

straight down—
which is the old back yard

When the child, successfully clutching the ball, hits "the old back yard," by God he is home.

Stevens' use of imagery is more airy than Williams', quite as the world of a part-time insurance man differs from the world of a part-time medical doctor, though each of these poets in his way is strongly aware of the appetites. That great "heavy" of Williams, "The Clouds," is interesting in this regard. The deathy horses, in a "charge from south to north" while a writhing black flag "fights/to be free," are racing in a gigantic turmoil (something like a visual analogue of Wagner's Valkyrs). It's a vision of such death as goes with fire, famine, plague and slaughter. That's how it starts. The second section is a kind of inventory, a quick sampling of the great dead, and done somewhat haphazardly, like glances at the scurrying clouds themselves. It brings the poet forcefully close to a vision of pure spirit despite himself: "The intellect leads, leads still! Beyond the clouds." Part three is a "scherzo," a kind of joke, grisly in this context, about a "holy man" who, while "riding/the clouds of his belief" (that is, officiating at a service) had "turned and grinned" at him. And the final stanza gets torn into unfinished uncertainty, quite like "the disordered heavens, ragged, ripped by winds." It is a gorgeous poem, at times almost ferocious, and stopped abruptly, in the middle of a sentence, as with the boy who had conscientiously caught the ball.

Elsewhere Williams aims at less drastic kinds of spirit, the most puzzling or puzzled contrivance being perhaps at the end of the long late poem, "Asphodel, that Greeny Flower." To be sure, the flower is green, and that's all to the good. But a few lines before the close we are informed, "Asphodel/has no odor/save to the imagination." Yet in an earlier poem we had been assured: "Time without/odor is Time without me." And one of Williams' most amusing early poems was an itemized rebuke to his nose for the "ardors" of its smelling.

At this point, another personal anecdote occurs to me, for its bearing upon Williams' character. On one occasion, when visiting us, he told me ruefully of misbehavior on his part (an incident that also falls under the head of "contact"). A little delegation of solemn admirers had come to pay him homage. Naturally, he was grateful to them. But as his poems overwhelmingly testify, he was also mercurial. And in the very midst of their solemnity at parting, since one of the little band happened to be a pretty young woman he gave her a frank, good-natured smack on the fanny. It was all part of the game, done on the spur of the moment, and it had seemed quite reasonable. It was the *tactus eruditus* in capricious relaxation.

But his visitors were horrified, and he realized that he had spoiled the whole show. He confessed to me his gloom at such unruly ways. But is it not a simple scientific fact that the poet they had come to honor owed much of his charm to precisely such whimsicality as this? One might class it with another occasion when, in a talk at a girls' school, he earnestly exhorted them, "You must learn to be a man." Maybe some of them did—but all were furious. How were they to be reminded precisely then that he was also the man who has written: "Anyone who has seen 2,000 infants born as I have and pulled them one way or another into the world must know that man, as such, is doomed to disappear in not too many thousand years. He just can't go on. No woman will stand for it. Why should she?"

I wish that, to commemorate Williams, some publisher would now reissue his *Al Que Quiere!*, just as it was in the original 1917 edition. It shows with such winsomeness this quirky aspect of his genius. Consider the crazy "Danse Russe," for intance, a poem delightfully alien to the pomposities that Eliot did so much to encourage; yet in their way the verse and prose of this "Diogenes" have been written into the very constitution of our country:

> If I when my wife is sleeping
> and the baby and Kathleen
> are sleeping
> and the sun is a flame-white disc
> in silken mists
> above shining trees,—
> if I in my north room
> dance naked, grotesquely
> before my mirror
> waving my shirt round my head
> and singing softly to myself:
> "I am lonely, lonely.
> I was born to be lonely.
> I am best so!"
> If I admire my arms, my face
> my shoulders, flanks, buttocks
> against the yellow drawn shades,—
>
> who shall say I am not
> the happy genius of my household?

Here also was first published the well-known "Tract," his instructions to his "townspeople," on "how to perform a funeral," lines

that were read by the minister, as a final goodbye, at the side of
Williams' own grave. That was exactly right. And at the end of the
book there is a long poem ("The Wanderer, a Rococo Study")
which, though it was written before the poet had fully got his
stride, and is a kind of romantic allegorizing that he would later
outlaw, yet is in its way notable, particularly as a stage in Williams'
development. For after several preparatory steps which it would
require too much space to detail here, it leads up to a ritualistic
transformation involving an imaginary baptism in the waters of
"The Passaic, that filthy river." These lines should be enough to
indicate how the merger of poet and physician initially involved a
somewhat magical process, thus:

> Then the river began to enter my heart,
> Eddying back cool and limpid
> Into the crystal beginning of its days.
> But with the rebound it leaped forward:
> Muddy, then black and shrunken
> Till I felt the utter depth of its rottenness
> The vile breath of its degradation
> And dropped down knowing this was me.

Here, surely, was the essential ritualistic step by which he began
his "contact" with "anti-poetry"—and though often, in later years,
he turned to the sheerly beautiful, even sheerly decorative, here we
see the tubes and coils and sluices of the powerhouse. Or am I but
tricked by the occasion into going back forty-plus years, and seeing
him too much as I saw him then? Yet recall (in *Journey to Love*)
that late poem, "The Sparrow," dedicated to his father, "a poetic
truth/more than a natural one," and thus a delightful contribution
to the *comédie humaine*. As you follow the great variety of *aperçus*
that use as their point of departure this busy mutt-bird, his ways
of congregation, his amours and family life, you heartily agree it's
"a pity/there are not more oats eaten/nowadays." Here is no less
than Aesop singing.

In the course of doing this piece, I found among my notes a let-
ter dated May 10, 1940. Presumably I had sent Williams some pages
which he had read with his usual mixture of friendliness and re-
sistance. He writes (enclosing a poem):

> If I hadn't been reading your essay and thinking my own thoughts
> against it—I shouldn't have stepped on the word "prebirth" and so
> the poem (completely independent of the whole matter otherwise)
> might not have been written.

THEREFORE the poem belongs to you. I like it as well as any-thing I have written—

Then, after some other matters, he returns to the subject abruptly: "All I wanted to do was to send you the poem."

At the time I assumed that he meant the gift figuratively. But after inquiring of John Thirlwall, who has spent so much effort tracking down Williams' scattered work, I think it possible that friendly Wm. C. Wms., strong man two-gun Bill, may have meant the gift literally, and I may possess the only copy of the poem. In any case, I append it here, since it is a lovely thing to end on. It has a kind of reversal which crops up somewhat mystically, every now and then, among his poems, and which is probably implicit in many other passages. In the light of such forms, when he writes "It is nearly pure luck that gets the mind turned inside out in a work of art," we may take it that he had such reversals in mind:

Cherry Blossoms at Evening

In the prebirth of the evening
the blue cherry blossoms
on the blue tree
from this yellow, ended room—
press to the windows
inside shall be out
the clustered faces of the flowers
straining to look in

(Signed) William Carlos Williams—

William Carlos Williams

by Wallace Stevens

I. *Preface to* Collected Poems, 1921-1931

The slightly tobaccoy odor of autumn is perceptible in these pages. Williams is past fifty.

There are so many things to say about him. The first is that he is a romantic poet. This will horrify him. Yet the proof is everywhere. Take the first poem, "All the Fancy Things." What gives this its distinction is the image of the woman, once a girl in Puerto Rico in the Old Spanish days, now solitary and growing old, not knowing what to do with herself, remembering. Of course, this is romantic in the accepted sense, and Williams is rarely romantic in the accepted sense.

The man has spent his life in rejecting the accepted sense of things. In that, most of all, his romantic temperament appears. But it is not enough merely to reject: what matters is the reason for rejection. The reason is that Williams has a romantic of his own. His strong spirit makes its own demands and delights to try its strength.

It will be observed that the lonely figure in "All the Fancy Things" and the person addressed in "Brilliant Sad Sun" have been slightly sentimentalized. In order to understand Williams at all, it is necessary to say at once that he has a sentimental side. Except for that, this book would not exist and its character would not be what it is. "The Cod Head" is a bit of pure sentimentalization; so is "The Bull." Sentiment has such an abhorrent name that one hesitates. But if what if what vitalizes Williams has an abhorrent name, its obviously generative function in his case may help to change its reputation. What Williams gives, on the whole, is not sentiment but the reaction from sentiment, or, rather, a little sentiment, very little, together with acute reaction.

His passion for the anti-poetic is a blood-passion and not a passion of the inkpot. The anti-poetic is his spirit's cure. He needs it as a naked man needs shelter or as an animal needs salt. To a man with a sentimental side the anti-poetic is that truth, that reality to which all of us are forever fleeing.

The anti-poetic has many aspects. The aspect to which a poet is addicted is a test of his validity. Its merely rhetorical aspect is valueless. As an affectation it is a commonplace. As a scourge it has a little more meaning. But as a phase of a man's spirit, as a source of salvation, now, in the midst of a baffled generation, as one looks out of the window at Rutherford or Passaic, or as one walks the streets of New York, the anti-poetic acquires an extraordinary potency, especially if one's nature possesses that side so attractive to the Furies.

Something of the unreal is necessary to fecundate the real; something of the sentimental is necessary to fecundate the anti-poetic. Williams, by nature, is more of a realist than is commonly true in the case of a poet. One might, at this point, set oneself up as the Linnæus of aesthetics, assigning a female role to the unused tent in "The Attic Which Is Desire," and a male role to the soda sign; and generally speaking one might run through these pages and point out how often the essential poetry is the result of the conjunction of the unreal and the real, the sentimental and the anti-poetic, the constant interaction of two opposites. This seems to define Williams and his poetry.

All poets are, to some extent, romantic poets. Thus, the poet who least supposes himself to be so is often altogether so. For instance, no one except a *surréaliste* himself would hesitate to characterize that whole school as romantic, dyed through and through with the most authentic purple. What, then, is a romantic poet nowadays? He happens to be one who still dwells in an ivory tower, but who insists that life would be intolerable except for the fact that one has, from the top, such an exceptional view of the public dump and the advertising signs of Snider's Catsup, Ivory Soap and Chevrolet Cars; he is the hermit who dwells alone with the sun and moon, but insists on taking a rotten newspaper. While Williams shares a good deal of this with his contemporaries in the manner and for the reason indicated, the attempt to define him and his work is not to be taken as an attempt to define anyone or anything else.

So defined, Williams looks a bit like that grand old plaster cast,

Lessing's Laocoön: the realist struggling to escape from the serpents of the unreal.

He is commonly identified by externals. He includes here specimens of abortive rhythms, words on several levels, ideas without logic, and similar minor matters, which, when all is said, are merely the diversions of the prophet between morning and evening song. It will be found that he has made some veritable additions to the corpus of poetry, which certainly is no more sacred to anyone than to him. His special use of the anti-poetic is an example of this. The ambiguity produced by bareness is another. The implied image, as in "Young Sycamore," the serpent that leaps up in one's imagination at his prompting, is an addition to imagism, a phase of realism which Williams has always found congenial. In respect to manner he is a virtuoso. He writes of flowers exquisitely. But these things may merely be mentioned. Williams himself, a kind of Diogenes of contemporary poetry, is a much more vital matter. The truth is that, if one had not chanced to regard him as Laocoön, one could have done very well by him as Diogenes.

II. *Rubbings of Reality*

If a man writes a little every day, as Williams does, or used to do, it may be that he is merely practicing in order to make perfect. On the other hand he may be practicing in order to get at his subject. If his subject is, say, a sense, a mood, an integration, and if his representation is faint or obscure, and if he practices in order to overcome his faintness or obscurity, what he really does is to bring, or try to bring, his subject into that degree of focus at which he sees it, for a moment, as it is and at which he is able to represent it in exact definition.

A man does not spend his life doing this sort of thing unless doing it is something he needs to do. One of the sanctions of the writer is that he is doing something that he needs to do. The need is not the desire to accomplish through writing something not incidental to the writing itself. Thus a political or a religious writer writes for political or religious reasons. Williams writes, I think, in order to write. He needs to write.

What is the nature of this need? What does a man do when he delineates the images of reality? Obviously, the need is a general need and the activity a general activity. It is of our nature that we proceed from the chromatic to the clear, from the unknown to the known. Accordingly the writer who practices in order to make perfect is really practicing to get at his subject and, in that exercise, is participating in a universal activity. He is obeying his nature. Imagism (as one of Williams' many involvements, however long ago) is not something superficial. It obeys an instinct. Moreover, imagism is an ancient phase of poetry. It is something permanent. Williams is a writer to whom writing is the grinding of a glass, the polishing of a lens by means of which he hopes to be able to see clearly. His delineations are trials. They are rubbings of reality.

The modern world is the result of such activity on a grand scale, not particularly in writing but in everything. It may be said, for instance, that communism is an effort to improve the human focus. The work of Picasso is an attempt to get at his subject, an attempt to achieve a reality of the intelligence. But the world of the past was equally the result of such activity. Thus the German pietists of the early 1700's who came to Pennsylvania to live in the caves of the Wissahickon and to dwell in solitude and meditation were proceeding in their way, from the chromatic to the clear. Is not Williams in a sense a literary pietist, chastening himself, incessantly, along the Passaic?

There is an intellectual *tenue*. It is easy to see how underneath the chaos of life today and at the bottom of all the disintegrations there is the need to see, to understand: and, in so far as one is not completely baffled, to re-create. This is not emotional. It springs from the belief that we have only our own intelligence on which to rely. This manifests itself in many ways, in every living art as in every living phase of politics or science. If we could suddenly re-make the world on the basis of our own intelligence, see it clearly and represent it without faintness or obscurity, Williams' poems would have a place there.

Poetry of Feeling

by Yvor Winters

W. C. Williams, in his view of life and of poetry, is an uncompromising romantic. He believes in the surrender to feeling and to instinct as the only way to wisdom and to art: "The Trees" is one of his many explicit statements of this notion. He believes that art is the product of a character which is "automatically first-rate" (*Blues* for May 1929). Such a character would have, of course, no need for ideas and no awareness of them; indeed, one may ask whether he would display any consciousness whatever. In any event, Dr. Williams distrusts all ideas and seeks value as far as may be in the concrete: in the poem called "Paterson" he reiterates the phrase "no ideas but in things." And he distrusts the entire range of feeling which is immediately motivated by ideas, for he is in no position to distinguish good ideas from bad, and hence, in this realm, sound feelings from false. In "A Poem for Norman McLeod," he writes: "The revolution/is accomplished/noble has been/changed to no bull." Any feeling arising from the contemplation of an idea, whether moral, metaphysical, or religious, appears to him merely sentimental: this is a defect, but he at least displays the virtue of his defect and almost wholly eschews the realm of experience which he does not understand, so that his poetry, though in certain ways limited, is at its best not confused or sentimental. He distrusts traditional form, as a kind of restraint or inhibition: since he fails to grasp its significance, it appears to him another mechanical sentimentalism; and he desires that the theme create its own form. But in this desire he has in part fallen short of his ambition, for his own excellent ear has made of free verse a complex accentual meter, very difficult to control, and creating very binding conventions of feeling.

His poetry therefore concentrates on the concrete; the only ideas which it occasionally expresses are those which I have outlined, and since the ideas are bad, the poetry is best when Dr. Williams follows his favorite formula and eschews ideas altogether. At its simplest, it resembles nearly all of his prose: that is, it offers merely sharp impressions of objects observed, either in isolation, or in accidental sequence, or forced by a purely rhetorical violence, as in "Romance Moderne," into a formal and emotional unit. In such a case as this last—and there are many such—the form, or emotion, which enacts the violence is unmotivated, and the whole effect, in spite of much brilliant detail, is one of excited overstatement. Some of the simplest, and purely isolated, descriptive notes are among the best; as for example, many of those in the sequence called "January Morning"; and occasionally, as in "Complaint," by virtue, perhaps, of some metrical or otherwise rhetorical miracle, one will take on inexplicable power. Dr. Williams' belief in this kind of thing no doubt accounts for his own high opinion of the poem about the red wheelbarrow in the rain, as compared to his other and often more valuable poems. Often his confidence in the intrinsic value of the physical object results in a poem composed of perfectly unrelated items, a passage of crystalline chaos, amusing but empty, as in the sixth poem of "Descent of Winter." He has not been without doubts in this connection, however; in "This Florida: 1924," he writes: "And we thought to escape rime/by imitation of the senseless/unarrangement of wild things—/the stupidest rime of all."

His theory, however, seems to permit his dealing with certain richer material; that is, with some of the simpler events of human relationship, chiefly love, seen primarily as something deeply desired but which passes. The best of these poems is probably "The Widow's Lament in Springtime," a poem both rich and somber, and one of the most moving compositions of our time. There are many others nearly as fine, among them "The Bull," "A Coronal," "Arrival," "Portrait of a Lady," "The Hunter," "The Lonely Street," "To Mark Anthony in Heaven," "To Waken An Old Lady," and "Waiting." In spite of the simplicity of theme, when the poems are viewed in bare outline, the sensuous and emotional awareness is extremely rich and is perfectly controlled; in style, the poems are masterly.

Here and there something else occurs that is even more impressive. His romantic view of nature and of art results in his experimenting with symbols of elemental forces and instincts. When, as in "The Trees," he passes an explicit judgment on these symbols in relationship to the intellectual values which he misapprehends and derides, the result is sentimental and essentially unsatisfactory. When, however, he represents the force in isolation, defining merely the power and the terror, he is perfectly sound and defensible; on at least three occasions, he has succeeded brilliantly with such symbols: in *Spring and All,* No. I ("On the road to the contagious hospital") and No. XXVI ("The crowd at the ball game"), and in "The Sea-Elephant." In these poems the violence of the theme supports even his most rapid and muscular rhetoric, and he raises the metrics of free verse and poetry in free verse to the highest level at which they may be found. No other poet using free verse is even comparable to him on these occasions.

The romantic principles which have governed Dr. Williams' work have limited his scope in the ways which I have mentioned. The combination of purity and of richly human feeling to be found in his language at times reminds one of Hardy or of Bridges, and in beauty of execution he is their equal, though in so different a mode; but his understanding is narrower than theirs, and his best poems are less great. On the other hand, when poems are so nearly unexceptionable in their execution, one regards the question of scope regretfully: Herrick is less great than Shakespeare, but he is probably as fine, and, God willing, should last as long. If I may venture, like Arnold, to make a prediction, it is this: that Williams will prove as nearly indestructible as Herrick; that the end of the present century will see him securely established, along with Stevens, as one of the two best poets of his generation. He is handicapped at present by the fact that the critical appreciation of free verse has not got beyond the long and somewhat obvious rhythms of Pound and of the less expert Eliot, so that Williams' artistry goes all but unperceived with most readers.

The present collection contains 313 pages and nearly all of Williams' poems.[1] There are no regrettable omissions that I can discover; there are few omissions of any kind. There are no poems butchered by hasty revision at the last minute, and a few that were so butchered in previous volumes have been repaired. The book is essentially complete and definitive, and it brings the author's work down to date. It is thus indispensable to anyone seriously concerned with American poetry. In regard to physical appearance, the book is beautifully and durably made, without being in any way pretentious; it is a luxury to handle it after having dealt for twenty years or so with the other volumes in which many of these poems have appeared.

[1] This essay was written as a review of *The Complete Collected Poems of William Carlos Williams, 1906-1938* (Norfolk, Conn.: New Directions Publishing Corporation, 1938).

IN POSTSCRIPT:

The preceding essay was written more than twenty-five years ago. My general remarks may stand, but by this time, I would restrict my choice of successful poems much more narrowly. "The Sea-Elephant" and "The crowd at the ball game" display Williams' foolish and sentimental ideas much too nakedly and can hardly be called successful. "The Widow's Lament" and others like it now strike me as soft, although charming in a gentle way; they are perhaps too obviously influenced by Pound's *Cathay*. The best poems, I feel sure, are these three from *Sour Grapes* (1921): "To Waken An Old Lady," "Complaint," and "The Great Figure"; and these two from *Spring and All* (1923): "By the road to the contagious hospital," and "Pink confused with white" ("The Pot of Flowers"). These are all minor poems, most of them very minor indeed, but they come close to perfection in execution. If I were to name another, it would be "The Hunter" from *Sour Grapes,* but it is a trifle florid as compared to those I have mentioned. To say that Williams was anti-intellectual would be almost an exaggeration: he did not know what the intellect was. He was a foolish and ignorant man, but at moments a fine stylist.

Y.W., 1965

The Unicorn in Paterson:
William Carlos Williams

by Louis L. Martz

This is the first part of a long poem in four parts—that a man in himself is a city, beginning, seeking, achieving and concluding his life in ways which the various aspects of a city may embody—if imaginatively conceived—any city, all the details of which may be made to voice his most intimate convictions. Part One introduces the elemental character of the place. The Second Part will comprise the modern replicas. Three will seek a language to make them vocal, and Four, the river below the falls, will be reminiscent of episodes— all that any one man may achieve in a lifetime.

So, in 1946, in his sixty-third year, Dr. Williams introduced the first part of his long poem *Paterson*, "a gathering up" of a lifetime's devotion to the poetical aim set for himself forty years before, when in his early poem, "The Wanderer," he dedicated his muse to "The Passaic, that filthy river."

> Then the river began to enter my heart,
> Eddying back cool and limpid
> Into the crystal beginning of its days.
> But with the rebound it leaped forward:
> Muddy, then black and shrunken
> Till I felt the utter depth of its rottenness . . .
> And dropped down knowing this was me now.
> But she lifted me and the water took a new tide
> Again into the older experiences,
> And so, backward and forward,
> It tortured itself within me
> Until time had been washed finally under,
> And the river had found its level

And its last motion had ceased
And I knew all—it became me.

Steadily, tenaciously, amid the multifold demands of a medical career, the books of *Paterson* appeared: and in 1951 the promised four books stood complete, fulfilling the wanderer's goal, and carrying out exactly the four-part design announced in Book I.

No wonder, then, that some admirers of *Paterson* were struck with consternation and dismay, a few years later, at the news that a *fifth* book of *Paterson* was in progress! That four-part design, so carefully announced and explained by the poet on several occasions—was it to be discarded now? To say the least, the whole procedure was inconsiderate of those critics who had published careful explanations of the poem's symmetry—and encouraging to those other critics who had felt that Book IV did not fulfill the poem's brilliant beginning. But, as usual, Williams knew exactly what he was doing. When, in 1958, the threatened Book V at last appeared, it proved to be an epilogue or coda, considerably shorter than the other books, and written in a reminiscent mode that served to recapitulate and bind together all the foregoing poem. As Williams himself wrote on the dust jacket of Book V: "I had to take the world of Paterson into a new dimension if I wanted to give it imaginative validity. Yet I wanted to keep it whole, as it is to me."

The chief agent and symbol of that wholeness is one that may at first seem incongruous with Williams' lifetime dedication to the local, his persistent refusal to adopt or approve the learned, foreign allusions of Ezra Pound or T. S. Eliot: in Book V the organizing symbol is the series of matchless tapestries in "The Cloisters" representing "The Hunt of the Unicorn." True, Williams had dealt briefly with these tapestries in the third book of *Paterson:*

> A tapestry hound
> with his thread teeth drawing crimson from
> the throat of the unicorn

But there the allusion to the world of traditional art seemed ironically overwhelmed by the surrounding scenes of basement ugliness and the fighting between "the guys from Paterson" and "the guys from Newark." Literally, it is only a short drive from Paterson to "The Cloisters"—but the gap of nearly five hundred years, the distance from France to the Passaic—these are dimensions strange to Williams, however familiar they may be to Pound or Eliot. But an afternoon spent with the great tapestries will show once more the canniness and subtlety of Williams' poetical strategies in *Paterson.*

Williams is defending and explaining his own technique by suggesting an analogy with the mode of the tapestries; and however unlikely any similarity may at first appear, the essential kinship is truly there. For these tapestries, like *Paterson,* achieve their success through a peculiar combination of the local and the mythical. We have the one hundred and one trees, shrubs, herbs, and flowers so realistically woven that eighty-five of them have been identified by botanists and praised for the exactitude of their reproduction; the "millefleurs background" is not composed of merely symbolical designs, but the colors burst forth from the actual, recognizable violet, cornflower, daisy, calendula, or dandelion. Yet all this actuality serves to border and center the mythical beast of oriental legend, serves to enfold and surround the human figures, the dogs, birds, and wild beasts, the castles and streams, the spears and hunting horns that crowd the scenes with a happy disregard of perspective—even to the point where the sixth tapestry superimposes the wounding of the unicorn upon an upper corner of the larger scene where the mythical beast is presented dead before the King and Queen. Meanwhile, amid the brilliant distortions of art and the splendor of color in flowers and costume, we find the brutal faces of certain varlets, the dog gutted by the unicorn's horn, the dog biting the unicorn's back, the vicious spears stabbing the "milk-white beast," the slanting, provocative, betraying eyes of the female attendant upon the virgin.

> . cyclamen, columbine, if the art
> with which these flowers have been
> put down is to be trusted—and
> again oak leaves and twigs
> that brush the deer's antlers . .
>
> > the brutish eyes of the deer
> > not to be confused
> > with the eyes of the Queen
> > are glazed with death .
>
> . a rabbit's rump escaping
> through the thicket .
>
> . . . .
>
> > a tapestry
> silk and wool shot with silver threads
> > a milk white one horned beast
> > > I, Paterson, the King-self
> saw the lady
> > through the rough woods
> > > outside the palace walls

                among the stench of sweating horses
                        and gored hounds
                                yelping with pain
            the heavy breathing pack
                    to see the dead beast
                            brought in at last
            across the saddle bow
                    among the oak trees.

The placing of that line, "I, Paterson, the King-self," implies a parallel between "Paterson," the poet, man, self, and city of the poem, and the Unicorn. The mythical beast is the spirit of the imagination, the immortal presence of art:

                            The Unicorn
        has no match
                or mate . the artist
                        has no peer .
        . . . .
        So through art alone, male and female, a field of
        flowers, a tapestry, spring flowers unequaled
        in loveliness.
                    through this hole
                    at the bottom of the cavern
                    of death, the imagination
                    escapes intact
            . he bears a collar round his neck
                    hid in the bristling hair.

Thus in the last of the series, the most famous of the tapestries, the Unicorn appears in peaceful resurrection. So "Paterson" now writes "In old age"—the opening line of Book V—and knows the threat of mortality as well as the reassurance promised by everything that the Unicorn represents—as we learn from the long closing passage dominated by the tapestries:

            —the aging body
                    with the deformed great-toe nail
        makes itself known
                    coming
                            to search me out—with a
                            rare smile
        among the thronging flowers of that field
                    where the Unicorn
                            is penned by a low

wooden fence
          in April!

· ·

the cranky violet
          like a knight in chess,
                    the cinque-foil,
yellow faced—
          this is a French
                    or Flemish tapestry—
the sweetsmelling primrose
          growing close to the ground, that poets
          have made famous in England,
                    I cannot tell it all:
slippered flowers
          crimson and white,
                    balanced to hang
on slender bracts, cups evenly arranged upon a stem,
          fox glove, the eglantine
                    or wild rose,
pink as a lady's ear lobe when it shows
          beneath the hair,
                    campanella, blue and purple tufts
small as forget-me-not among the leaves.
          Yellow centers, crimson petals
                    and the reverse,
dandelion, love-in-a-mist,
          corn flowers,
                    thistle and others
the names and perfumes I do not know.
          The woods are filled with holly
                    (I have told you, this
is a fiction, pay attention),
          the yellow flag of the French fields is here
                    and a congeries of other flowers
as well: daffodils
          and gentian, the daisy, columbine
                    petals
myrtle, dark and light
          and calendulas .

Anyone who reads the excellent pamphlet on the flora of the tapes-
tries provided by the museum will see at once that most of the flowers
here included by Williams are clearly recognizable and listed under

these names; but the poet is not presenting a catalogue: he is re-creating the act of personal, immediate, imaginative apprehension. Thus at times the poet gives his own familiar names, draws his own conclusions, imagines likenesses. The "myrtle, dark and light," for instance, must be the "periwinkle *(Vinca)*" which "appears only in the two normal colors of white and blue." And the "cinque-foil,/yellow faced" is not mentioned in the museum's account, but it is not hard to find it suggested by certain flowers. Most important, the familiar, intimate quality of the poet's account reminds us that many of these flowers have appeared in the dozens of flower-poems and the hundreds of flower-images scattered throughout the poetry of William Carlos Williams, from his early tributes to the daisy, the primrose, and the "yellow cinque-foil," down through the great tribute to Demuth, "The Crimson Cyclamen," and on into the recent long flower-tribute to his wife: "Asphodel, That Greeny Flower," where the poet recalls his boyhood collection of "pressed flowers." Williams is one of the great poets of flowers and foliage, which he observes and represents with a loving and a scientific accuracy akin to that of the Unicorn tapestries. Indeed, in a passage typical of *Paterson's* mode of organization, this fifth book itself reminds us from the outset of the poet's personal love of flowers by including on its fourth page a personal letter to "Dear Bill":

> I wish you and F. could have come. It was a grand day and we missed you two, one and all missed you. Forgetmenot, wild columbine, white and purple violets, white narcissus, wild anemonies and yards and yards of delicate wild windflowers along the brook showed up at their best. . . .

> How lovely to read your memories of the place; a place is made of them as well as the world around it. Most of the flowers were put in many years ago and thrive each spring, the wild ones in some new spot that is exciting to see. Hepaticas and bloodroot are now all over the place, and the trees that were infants are now tall creatures filled this season with orioles, some rare warbler like the Myrtle and magnolia warblers and a wren has the best nest in the garage. . . .[1]

So the new Book V suggests that we might regard *Paterson* as a kind of tapestry, woven out of memories and observations, composed by one man's imagination, but written in part by his friends, his patients, and all the milling populace of Paterson, past and present;

---

[1] This letter (signed "Josie") seems to allude to Williams' memories of the farm owned by Josephine Herbst and her husband, John Herrmann: see his account of the place in *The Autobiography of William Carlos Williams* (New York: Random House, 1951), pp. 269-71.

letters from Williams' friends are scattered amply throughout the poem: Book V devotes a whole page to transcribing a letter from Ezra Pound.

The whole, as Williams insists, is a "fiction" ("pay attention"), but it is at the same time a personal testament to the poet's vehement belief "that there is a source *in America* for everything we think or do." Why, then, he asks, "Why should I move from this place/where I was born?"—Rutherford, New Jersey, next door to Paterson.[2]

II

To find the source, to discover the place—in America—has been his lifelong aim. Thus we have heard now for about forty years Williams' warm, friendly, admiring, generous disagreement with the poetical directions of his lifelong friend Ezra Pound ("The best enemy United States verse has," he once declared).[3] And so too, in quite a different tone, we have heard Williams' rasping antagonism toward the achievement of T. S. Eliot. The publication of *The Waste Land*, he declares in his *Autobiography*, was "the great catastrophe to our letters":

> There was heat in us, a core and a drive that was gathering headway upon the theme of a rediscovery of a primary impetus, the elementary principle of all art, in the local conditions. Our work staggered to a halt for a moment under the blast of Eliot's genius which gave the poem back to the academics. We did not know how to answer him.

> Critically Eliot returned us to the classroom just at the moment when I felt that we were on the point of an escape to matters much closer to the essence of a new art form itself—rooted in the locality which should give it fruit. . . .

> If with his skill he could have been kept here to be employed by our slowly shaping drive, what strides might we not have taken! . . . By his walking out on us we were stopped, for the moment, cold. It was a bad moment. Only now, as I predicted, have we begun to catch hold again . . . (pp. 146, 174).[4]

[2] *In the American Grain* (New York: New Directions Publishing Corporation, 1956), p. 109; *Paterson*, Books I-IV (New York: New Directions Publishing Corporation, 1953), p. 93. Subsequent page references to these works allude to these editions. In the first editions the pages of *Paterson* are not numbered, perhaps in order to stress the plastic and non-logical organization of the poem.

[3] In the Prologue to *Kora in Hell* (1920), reprinted in Williams' *Selected Essays* (New York: Random House, 1954), p. 24.

[4] Eliot was somewhat more generous in his attitude toward Williams. On February 15, 1959, he wrote to the young American poet and critic, Richard

In those words, published in the same year as the fourth book of *Paterson,* we have a clue to one aspect of that poem's whole design. The more we read and reread *Paterson,* the more it emerges as a subtly devised protest against the cosmopolitan, the learned, the foreign aspects of such poems as *The Waste Land, Four Quartets,* and *The Cantos.* This is made especially plain near the end of the first book of *Paterson,* where Williams writes:

> Moveless
> he envies the men that ran
> and could run off
> toward the peripheries—
> to other centers, direct—
> for clarity (if
> they found it)
>   loveliness and
> authority in the world—
>
> a sort of springtime
> toward which their minds aspired
> but which he saw,
> within himself—ice bound
>
> and leaped, "the body, not until
> the following spring, frozen in
> an ice cake."   (p. 48)

It is a leap from the Falls: one of the major symbols of the poem; and whether or not the poet, like old Sam Patch, the daring diver, perishes at the river's bottom, the descent must be made:

> Caught (in mind)
> beside the water he looks down, listens!
> But discovers, still, no syllable in the confused
> uproar: missing the sense (though he tries)
> untaught but listening, shakes with the intensity
> of his listening.   (p. 100)

A. Macksey, whose essay on Williams is included elsewhere in this volume. "Poetry," said Eliot of Williams, "springs from the most unexpected soil. . . . He continues to split rocks and find poems." This way of putting it is elegantly apt, for Eliot here echoes motifs fundamental to Williams' thought: the image of flowering, the image of saxifrage, and the image of poetry as a radiant gist buried in rock. (The copyright for T. S. Eliot's letter is held by Mrs. T. S. Eliot; permission to quote from it has been granted by Mrs. T. S. Eliot and Richard A. Macksey.) [ED.]

It is a descent, through memory, to the sources of the self, as Williams makes clear in a passage from the second book of *Paterson* (p. 96)—a passage that later appeared as the opening poem of his collection, *The Desert Music* (1954) :

> The descent beckons
>   as the ascent beckoned.
>   Memory is a kind
> of accomplishment,
>   a sort of renewal
>   even
> an initiation, since the spaces it opens are new places
>   inhabited by hordes
>   heretofore unrealized,
> of new kinds—
>   since their movements
>   are towards new objectives
> (even though formerly they were abandoned)

Thus *Paterson* becomes the full realization of the moral vision, the literary theory, the aesthetic manifesto, set forth in the best of his earlier works, *In the American Grain* (1925). We must not mistake this book for an interpretation of history, although it deals with Montezuma, de Soto, Raleigh, Daniel Boone, and George Washington, and although it contains excerpts from the journals of Columbus and from the writings of Cotton Mather, Ben Franklin, and John Paul Jones. The point is not history but rather a search in the memory of America to discover, to invent, symbols of the ideals from which Williams' life and writings have developed.

In the American Grain works with American figures, but the basic issues of the book are universal. It seeks a way of moving from an old world into a new; it seeks a way of leaving the finished forms of culture and dealing with the roar, the chaos, of the still-to-be-achieved. The book discerns two modes of treating the problem. One is found in Williams' version of the Puritan, who represents here, not a single religious creed, but the way of all men who lack "the animate touch" (p. 177), and who therefore set up within themselves a "resistance to the wilderness" which is the new life all about them pp. (115-16).

In contrast to this view, with "its rigid clarity, its *inhuman* clarity, its steel-like thrust from the heart of each isolate man straight into the tabernacle of Jehovah" (p. 111), Williams presents another vision, dramatized by a group of great explorers, sensitive to the wonder of the life all about them in the new world. There is Columbus, who on the twelfth of October found a world that was filled with things "wonderful," "handsome," "marvelous," "beautiful." "During that time I walked among the trees which was the most beautiful thing which I had ever seen . . ." (pp. 25-26). They are the very words which twenty-five years later Williams recalls in the fourth book of *Paterson* (p. 209), thus picking up the phrase "beautiful thing" which has formed the theme of his poem's third book. And we have Cortez, Ponce de Leon, de Soto, Raleigh, and Champlain, "like no one else about him, watching, keeping the thing whole within him with almost a woman's tenderness—but such an energy for detail—a love of the exact detail—" (pp. 69-70).

In these explorers Williams finds a quality of wonder utterly different from what is found in Cotton Mather's "Wonders of the Invisible World," his defense of the Salem witchcraft trials, from which Williams here provides long extracts. In Cotton Mather's own words, the Puritans "embraced a voluntary Exile in a squallid, horrid American Desart"; they felt themselves "a People of God settled in those, which were once the *Devil's* Territories" (pp. 82-83). *In the American Grain* then turns from these accounts of witchcraft to a chapter entitled "Père Sebastian Rasles," but sixteen pages pass before we meet this missionary to the Indians of Maine. Instead we are moved abruptly from Cotton Mather to the Parisian world of the 1920s, where we find Williams surrounded by Picasso, Gertrude Stein, the Prince of Dahomi, James and Norah Joyce, Bryher, H. D., "dear Ezra," and other expatriates. Williams is discussing with Valéry Larbaud the situation of the American writer. "What we are," he argues, "has its origin in what *the nation* in the past has been . . . unless everything that is, proclaim a ground on which it stand, it has no worth . . . what has been morally, aesthetically worth while in America has rested upon peculiar and discoverable ground" (p. 109). And in that ground, he declares, we find "two flaming doctrines" (p. 127). One is Williams' version of the Puritan, and the other is that represented by Rasles, who here becomes a symbol of a way of life maintained by the animate touch. For thirty-four years, says Williams, this French Jesuit lived among his Indians, "*touching* them every day." In Rasles Williams discovers "a spirit, rich, blossoming, generous, able to give and to receive, full of taste, a nose, a tongue, a laugh, enduring, self-forgetful in beneficence—a new spirit in the New World." His vision of life as imagined by Williams is one the poet can share: "Nothing shall be ignored. All shall be included. The world is parcel of the Church so that every leaf, every vein in every leaf, the throbbing of the temples is of that mysterious flower. Here is richness, here is color, here is form." "Reading his letters, it is a river that brings sweet water to us. *This* is a moral source not reckoned with, peculiarly sensitive and daring in its close embrace of native things" (pp. 120-21).

What does it all mean set thus in Paris, amid exiles gathered from England, Africa, Spain, Ireland, and especially America? These exiles, it seems, must be a modern version of the Puritans. They are those who have felt themselves living in a "squallid, horrid American Desart"; they have refused, like Cotton Mather, to embrace the wilderness. Williams turns instead to those like Daniel Boone, who, says Williams, "lived to enjoy ecstasy through his single devotion to the wilderness with which he was surrounded"; like Rasles, Boone sought "to explore always more deeply, to see, to feel, to touch . . ." (p. 136). For Williams, the trouble with modern American culture is that the meaning of life has been obscured "by a field of unrelated culture stuccoed upon it," obscured by what he calls "the aesthetic adhesions of the present day" (p. 212). He seeks instead the "impact of the bare soul upon the very twist of the fact which is our world about us" (p. 178). For in this impact, the poet (in us all) discovers or invents the beautiful thing. True, the new world no longer holds "the orchidean beauty" that Cortez, "overcome with wonder," saw in Montezuma's Mexico: "Streets, public squares, markets, temples, palaces, the city spread its dark life upon the earth of a new world, rooted there, sensitive to its richest beauty, but so completely removed from those foreign contacts which harden and protect, that at the very breath of conquest it vanished" (pp. 27, 30, 31-32). True, we have instead the city—Paterson—that has resulted from the schemes of Alexander Hamilton: "Paterson he wished to make capital of the country because there was waterpower there which to his time and mind seemed colossal. And so he organized a company to hold the land thereabouts, with dams and sluices, the origin today of the vilest swillhole in christendom, the Passaic River . . ." (p. 195). For all this, Williams argues, we must still, like Boone and Houston, make "a descent to the ground" of our desire (p. 136). "However hopeless it may seem, we have no other choice: we must go back to the beginning . . ." (p. 215).[5]

III

From this bare ground Williams then begins his *Paterson;* an answer to those "who know all the Latin and some of the Sanskrit

[5] The foregoing discussion of *In the American Grain* echoes a few paragraphs in my earlier article, "William Carlos Williams: On the Road to Paterson," *Poetry New York*, No. 4 (1951), pp. 18-32.

names" (*Grain,* p. 214). Williams prepares his answer in a way subtly suggested by a passage in the second book of *Paterson,* where he seems to echo wryly one of the most famous passages of Pound, Canto 45, on usury, where Pound adopts the manner of a medieval or a renaissance preacher:

> With usura hath no man a house of good stone
> each block cut smooth and well fitting
> that design might cover their face,
> with usura
> hath no man a painted paradise on his church wall
> *harpes et luthes* . . .
>
> with usura the line grows thick
> with usura is no clear demarcation
> and no man can find site for his dwelling.
> Stone cutter is kept from his stone
> weaver is kept from his loom . . .
>
> Came not by usura Angelico; came not Ambrogio Praedis,
> Came no church of cut stone signed: *Adamo me fecit* . . .
>
> Usura rusteth the chisel
> It rusteth the craft and the craftsman
> It gnaweth the thread in the loom
> None learneth to weave gold in her pattern . . .

And now this from *Paterson:*

> Without invention nothing is well spaced,
> unless the mind change, unless
> the stars are new measured, according
> to their relative positions, the
> line will not change . . .
>
>   without invention
> nothing lies under the witch-hazel
> bush, the alder does not grow from among
> the hummocks margining the all
> but spent channel of the old swale,
> the small foot-prints
> of the mice under the overhanging
> tufts of the bunch-grass will not
> appear: without invention the line
> will never again take on its ancient

> divisions when the word, a supple word,
> lived in it, crumbled now to chalk.   (p. 65)

What does this contrast say of these two poets at their best? Williams' own critical acuteness gives us the answer in one of his letters of 1932:

> So far I believe that Pound's line in his *Cantos*—there is something *like* what we shall achieve. Pound in his mould, a medieval inspiration, patterned on a substitution of medieval simulacra for a possible, not yet extant modern and living material, has made a pre-composition for us. Something which when later (perhaps) packed and realized in living, breathing stuff will (in its changed form) be the thing.[6]

It is a summary of Williams' achievement in *Paterson:* the mold is Pound's, combining verse and prose; the line is Pound's, with its flexible cadences, breaking the pentameter; but everything is altered through Williams' invention, his conviction that bold exploration of the local will result in the discovery of a new world blossoming all about him. Pound's mind lives at its best among the splendors of ancient human artifacts, and when these splendors seem threatened, Pound seeks a social answer. He seeks to make art possible by reforming the economic basis of society. It is a difference between the two friends that Pound has acutely described in his essay on Williams (1928), as he contrasts their two temperaments: "If he wants to 'do' anything about what he sees, this desire for action does not rise until he has meditated in full and at leisure. Where I see scoundrels and vandals, he sees a spectacle or an ineluctable process of nature. Where I want to kill at once, he ruminates." [7]

At the same time, in his ruminative way, Williams gradually implies some degree of sympathy with Pound's economic views. Among the prose passages of the second book of *Paterson,* we find attacks on the Federal Reserve System; we find, too, implied attacks on Alexander Hamilton's plans for federal financing and for creating a great "National Manufactory" powered by the Passaic falls. These prose excerpts on financial matters are interwoven with the poetical sermon of the evangelist who, in the second book of *Paterson,* delivers his sermon against money to the birds and trees of the park. But this financial theme, thus introduced, is tightly contained within this section: it lies there dormant, recessive, exerting a tacit pressure on the landscape, until, in the center of Book IV, it bursts

[6] *The Selected Letters of William Carlos Williams,* ed. John C. Thirlwall (New York: Ivan Obolensky, Inc., 1957), p. 135.
[7] *Literary Essays of Ezra Pound,* ed. T. S. Eliot (London: Faber and Faber, Ltd., 1954), p. 392.

out again in a highly Poundian diatribe beginning "Money: Joke."
Here is a section composed in something like Pound's broken multi-
cultural style, with expressions in Hebrew, Spanish, and German,
along with very crude American slang; and including too some
allusions to the Parthenon, Phidias, and Pallas Athene—all this
ending with an overt echo of Pound's unmistakable epistolary style:

> IN
> venshun.
> O.KAY
> In venshun

(It sounds like Pound nodding his head to the passage on invention
that I have just quoted.)

> and seeinz az how yu hv/started. Will you consider
> a remedy of a lot:
> > i.e. LOCAL control of local purchasing
> > > power .
> > > > ? ?
> Difference between squalor of spreading slums
> and splendor of renaissance cities.   (p. 218)

It is a tribute to Pound, yes; but it is not for Williams to conclude
his own poem in this foreign vein, it is not for Williams to excoriate
the present and celebrate the "splendor of renaissance cities." This
is an invitation that Williams has already refused to accept in the
third book of *Paterson,* entitled "The Library," where we find the
poet attempting to discover a "sanctuary to our fears" amid the
"cool of books":

> A cool of books
> will sometimes lead the mind to libraries
> of a hot afternoon, if books can be found
> cool to the sense to lead the mind away.   (p. 118)

He is attempting to escape from the roar of that Falls which pro-
vides the central symbol of this poem, for the roar of the Falls in
his mind, "pouring down," has left him exhausted.

> . . . a falls unseen
> tumbles and rights itself
> and refalls—and does not cease, falling
> and refalling with a roar, a reverberation
> not of the falls but of its rumor
> > unabated.   (p. 119)

Here, the mysterious evocative symbol of the great Falls of the Passaic comes as close to clarity as we shall ever find it. It seems to represent the roar of human speech, the roar of human thought in the mind; it is the roar of the language coming down from the past, mingling with the present, and now bursting downward over the brain of "Paterson," who seeks to find somehow in that fall of speech, the beautiful thing that is the ground of his desire. *"What do I do? I listen, to the water falling. . . . This is my entire occupation"* (p. 60). But now he is

> Spent from wandering the useless
> streets these months, faces folded against
> him like clover at nightfall,

and he feels that somehow

> Books will give rest sometimes against
> the uproar of water falling
> and righting itself to refall filling
> the mind with its reverberation.   (pp. 118-19)

But it is not so. As he sits there reading "old newspaper files," old annals of Paterson—things like those prose passages of which his poem is in part compounded—as he reads, he finds the roar there, too: stories of fire, cyclone and flood that now beset the poet until his mind "reels, starts back amazed from the reading" (p. 120) —until the very poem threatens to break apart upon the page (see p. 164). Where to turn? What to do? In ironical answer, Williams brings in certain excerpts from a letter headed "S. Liz," that is, from St. Elizabeth's Hospital:

> re read *all* the Gk tragedies in
> Loeb.—plus Frobenius, plus Gesell.
> plus Brooks Adams
> ef you ain't read him all.—
> Then Golding's Ovid is in
> Everyman's lib.
>
> & nif you want a readin
> list ask papa—but don't
> go rushin to *read* a book
> just cause it is mentioned
> eng passang—is fraugs.   (p. 165)

Williams' answer to Pound is sly. On the next page, he prints an excerpt from some record evidently found in the Paterson Library concerning the drillings taken at the artesian well of the Passaic

Rolling Mill, Paterson, and as the results of this local rock-drill run down the page, the excerpt concludes with this significant suggestion: "The fact that the rock salt of England, and of some of the other salt mines of Europe, is found in rocks of the same age as this, raises the question whether it may not also be found here."

"Whether it may not also be found here." For Williams, it may, it can, it will be found here, as he proves by giving in the final section of Book IV a recovery of the source: the pastoral Paterson of early days at peace with the Falls.

> In a deep-set valley between hills, almost hid
> by dense foliage lay the little village.
> Dominated by the Falls the surrounding country
> was a beautiful wilderness where mountain pink
> and wood violet throve: a place inhabited only
> by straggling trappers and wandering Indians.
> . . . .
> Just off Gun Mill yard, on the gully
> was a long rustic winding stairs leading
> to a cliff on the opposite side of the river.
> At the top was Fyfield's tavern—watching
> the birds flutter and bathe in the little
> pools in the rocks formed by the falling
> mist—of the Falls . . .

Here is our home, says the poet, inland by the Falls and not in the outgoing sea, as Williams concludes in the rousing finale of Book IV:

> I warn you, the sea is *not* our home,
>   the sea is not our home

Here the sea appears to symbolize something more than simple death, national or personal annihilation. For this is also a sea where "float words, snaring the seeds":

>   the nostalgic sea
>   sopped with our cries
>   Thalassa! Thalassa!
>   calling us home .
>   I say to you, Put wax rather in your
>   ears against the hungry sea
>   it is not our home!
>   . draws us in to drown, of losses
>   and regrets .

The sea appears to represent the pull of longing toward a lost culture, a pull outward from the source, as he goes on to indicate by an overwrought cry that seems to parody the longing of a Pound or an Eliot:

> Oh that the rocks of the Areopagus had
> kept their sounds, the voices of the law!
> Or that the great theatre of Dionysius
> could be aroused by some modern magic
> . . . .
> Thalassa! Thalassa!
> > Drink of it, be drunk!
> > > Thalassa
> immaculata: our home, our nostalgic
> mother in whom the dead, enwombed again
> cry out to us to return   .

". . . not our home!" cries the poet again in violent protest, "It is NOT our home." And suddenly at the very close of this fourth book, the scene shifts, the tone shifts, to a common seashore with a man bathing in the sea, and his dog waiting for him on the beach.

> When he came out, lifting his knees
> through the waves she went to him frisking
> her rump awkwardly   .
> Wiping his face with his hand he turned
> to look back to the waves, then
> knocking at his ears, walked up
> to stretch out flat on his back in
> the hot sand   .

And finally after a brief nap and a quick dressing, the man

> > turned again
> to the water's steady roar, as of a distant
> waterfall   .   Climbing the
> bank, after a few tries, he picked
> some beach plums from a low bush and
> sampled one of them, spitting the seed out,
> then headed inland, followed by the dog

"Headed inland"—here at the very close, Williams echoes once again his prose preparation for this poem, *In the American Grain*, for in the closing pages of that earlier book, he had used the same phrasing to describe the achievement of Edgar Allan Poe. "His greatness," Williams there declared, "is in that he turned his back" upon everything represented by a Longfellow and "faced inland, to originality, with the identical gesture of a Boone" (p. 226). And indeed Williams' account here of Poe's method in his tales is perhaps the best account of *Paterson* that we have yet received:

> the significance and the secret is: authentic particles, a thousand of which spring to the mind for quotation, taken apart and reknit with a view to emphasize, enforce and make evident, the *method*. Their quality of skill in observation, their heat, local verity, being *overshadowed* only by the detached, the abstract, the cold philosophy of their joining together; a method springing so freshly from the local conditions which determine it, by their emphasis of firm crudity and lack of coordinated structure, as to be worthy of most painstaking study—   (pp. 230-31)

So the two major works of William Carlos Williams reinforce each other, while the tapestry of *Paterson* recalls the whole body of Williams' poetry, as now six pages from the end of Book V we hear:

> "the river has returned to its beginnings"
>   and backward
>   (and forward)
>   it tortures itself within me
>   until time has been washed finally under:
>   and "I knew all (or enough)
>   it became me   .   "

A Note on *The Great American Novel*

by Hugh Kenner

The pretensions inherent in the title are part of Dr. Williams' theme. The lad who was going to produce "The Great American Novel" as soon as he had gotten his mind around his adolescent experience is part of the folklore of the twenties, and the prevalence of this myth documents the awareness of the young American of thirty years ago that the consciousness of his race remained uncreated. The world of Henry James had always been special, and by now was long vanished; James apart, the job of articulating the American psyche remained about where Whitman had left it. Hence Williams' opening gesture:

The Great
American Novel

CHAPTER I.

THE FOG.

This is a parody of a beginner's beginning. It is also, though the beginner doesn't really know it, the place such a book should begin, because it is where the subject begins. (*"American poetry,"* the author of *Paterson* remarks, *"is a very easy subject to discuss for the simple reason that it does not exist."*) He continues, weaving in strands of Whitman, empty nature, monosyllabic primitivism, and the sort of brainless pretentiousness that is really too authentic to be a pretense:

> If there is progress then there is a novel. Without progress there is nothing. Everything exists from the beginning. I existed in the beginning. I was a slobbering infant. Today I saw nameless grasses—I tapped the earth with my knuckle. It sounded hollow. It was dry as

rubber. Eons of drought. No rain for fifteen days. No rain. It has
never rained. It will never rain. . . .

A kind of innocence inheres in the attempts of the Thomas
Wolfes and Ross Lockridges to swallow and regurgitate America
whole. If they or their 1920 forerunners corrupted their material
more there would be no point in parodying their gaggings and
flounderings:

> Break the words. Words are indivisible crystals. One cannot break
> them—Awu tsst grang splith gra pragh og bm—Yes, one can break
> them. One can make words. Progress? If I make a word I make myself
> into a word. One big word. One big union. Such is progress. It is a
> novel. I begin small and make myself into a big splurging word: I take
> life and make it into one big blurb. I begin at my childhood. I begin
> at the beginning and make one big—Bah.

This maintains a remarkable poise, midway between spoof and
earnestness. Yet the tone isn't genial, embracing these extremes, but
irascible, polarizing them. The irascibility thrusts two ways, at the
thankless job and at the entrail-searching of the Epigoni. The lat-
ter aren't disregarded or fended off as irrelevant, because their in-
choate state of mind is part of the subject. So is the careful realism
of a later paragraph:

> Leaving the meeting room where the Mosquito Extermination
> Commission had been holding an important fall conference they
> walked out on to the portico of the County Court House Annex
> where for a moment they remained in the shadow cast by the moon.
> . . . Coming to the car he said: Go around that side as I will have to
> get in here by the wheel. . . .

This is fashionable writing of the twenties, a notebook exercise. Its
studied awkwardness, however, is in touch not only with journalism
but with an authentic stratum of experience: a sleepwalking aware-
ness of the inconsequential. The European tradition has no idiom
for this state of consciousness, endemic among people who spend
a great deal of time operating machinery.

In the opening pages of the book, in fact, various fashionable
techniques and postures are being put to use as subject matter,
blocks of verbal material. Here is another specimen:

> . . . Clean, clean he had taken each word and made it new for him-
> self so that at last it was new, free from the world for himself—never
> to touch it—dreams of his babyhood—poetic sweetheart. No. He
> went in to his wife with exalted mind, his breath coming in pleasant
> surges. I come to tell you that the book is finished.
> I have added a new chapter to the art of writing. I feel sincerely

that all they say of me is true, that I am truly a great man and a great poet.

What did you say, dear, I have been asleep?

This doesn't parody *writing*. "He went in to his wife with exalted mind, his breath coming in pleasant surges": given the mood, a conceivable one, the words couldn't be better. It is the dream of a writer who hasn't written a word, and it parodies certain naïve motives for undertaking authorship which—once more—are part of Williams' subject. One can fancy the bloated abortion this "great man and great poet" might commit; in its place Williams offers a "Great American Novel" in exactly seventy pages of text, with no plot and no hero. And however often Williams prods lyrical themes, the words remain stunned. Though they go through all the motions of taking flight, they never bear the reader aloft. What the lyrical passages are about is ineffectual motions of flight. The afflatus of the young American romantic leads him to seek the elements of his subject in himself: hence the involuted values Williams is able to extract from the convention of a book about a man writing a book. On later pages, having exhausted the romantic's resources, Williams takes stock of a hundred modes of reality and vulgarity, also part of the subject, which no young poet will admit infest his soul.

One reason the words must be stunned is that the American language, or the part of it that interests Williams, is distinguished by a sort of amnesia. Though their colloquial vocabularies are restricted, their syntax simple, and their speech rhythms the reverse of Ciceronian, Americans don't utter a gelatinous Basic English. They have rhythmic and idiomatic means of concentrating meaning in these counters, shifting the burden of the sentence with a certain laconic grace from word to word, which falsifies the unthinking novelist's assumption that the way to extract the unuttered meanings of American experience is to assist these pidgin gropings with the fuller cadences of European prose. European prose, when it attempts to grapple with American material, yields nothing but suave cliché. At the beginning of Chapter XI a European voice protests,

> *Eh bien mon vieux coco,* this stuff that you have been writing today, do you mean that you are attempting to set down the American background? You will go mad. Why? Because you are trying to do nothing at all. The American background? It is Europe. It can be nothing else. . . .

This mind thinks in phrases, not in words: the upward lilt between its punctuation marks is the signature of a habit of apprehension shaped by Latin prose. A European would have imparted a more elegant rhythm to the answering sentence, which comes with Williams' own unmistakable flatness:

As far as I have gone it is accurate.

These shadings of "far," "gone," and "accurate" aren't in a European dictionary: they are imposed by the tractorlike cadence. "Accurate," in this sentence, has forgotten its Latin past ("L. *accuratus,* past part. & adj., fr. *accurare* to take care of, fr. *ad + curare* to take care, fr. *cura* care"). Its stress isn't verbal, reflecting the care that has been taken, but attributive, implying a scientific absolute achieved.

That the cadence in which words move controls the degree of meaning they yield up, and that words set in Jersey speech rhythms mean less but mean it with greater finality, is Williams' chief technical perception. It underlies his intricate, inelegant verse rhythms:

> —an old barn
> is peaked there also, fatefully,
> against the sky. And there it is
> and we can't shift it or change
> it or parse it or alter it
> in any way.

That "fatefully" has force but no plangence; and "parse" doesn't receive the deliberative stress that would make it a witty metaphor. It is the odd pointlessness with which the line division (always Williams' principal instrument) bisects "change/it" that flattens "parse" and all the adjacent words: a more delicate feat than it looks.

In *The Great American Novel* Williams' skill at exorcising from words the "pleasing wraiths of former masteries" interlocks with a number of aphorisms about the irrelevance of traditional fiction: "Permanence. A great army with its tail in antiquity. Cliché of the soul: beauty." . . . "Europe's enemy is the past. Our enemy is Europe, a thing unrelated to us in any way." Hence the systematic eschewal both of pseudo-Aristotelian plot with its stereotyped climax, and of pseudo-Roman fine writing with its spurious epithets and cadences. The subject yields no plot, but it implies a wide range of textures: Spanish explorers, Southern mountaineers, Aaron Burr, the Presbyterian minister in Bonnie, Illinois. No narrative, no analysis, nothing but a suitably balanced sensibility can hold them together. So the "Novel," bringing its lyric phases under progressively stricter control, acquires by cunning trial and error a reliable tone which in the final chapters can handle with a compositor's sureness a surprising variety of materials and effects: from "Particles of falling stars, coming to nothing. The air pits them, eating out the softer parts" to "The Perfection of Pisek-designed Personality Modes: A distinctly forward move in the realm of fashion is suggested by the new personality modes, designed by Pisek . . ."

At the end he returns to surer-footed parody. Coming after a survey of simple beginnings, the last two chapters ("Witness, O witness these lives my dainty cousins") borrow the journalist's congratulatory accents to suggest the apotheosis of commercial dreams:

> I had five cents in my pocket and a piece of apple pie in my hand, said Prof. M. I. Pupin, of Columbia University, describing the circumstances of his arrival in America in the steerage of the steamship Westphalie from Hamburg half a century ago.

One kind of Great American Novel, we remember, was written by Horatio Alger, the authentic folklorist of hustling America.

But the book doesn't close on this note of innocence; the climax, an interview with a successful rag merchant, rounds on Great American Novels and Great America alike:

> Why one man made a million before the government stopped him by making cheap quilts.
>
> He took any kind of rags just as they were collected, filth or grease right on them the way they were and teased them up into a fluffy stuff which he put through a rolling process and made into sheets of wadding. These sheets were fed mechanically between two layers of silkolene and a girl simply sat there with an electric sewing device which she guided with her hand and drew in the designs you see on those quilts, you know.
>
> You've seen this fake oilcloth they are advertising now. Congoleum. Nothing but building paper with a coating of enamel.
>
> ¡O vida tan dulce!

Fluffy stuff, sheets of wadding, the mechanical patterns: a host of metaphors for shoddy art emerge from a passage which, like the artesian-well page in *Paterson*, achieves its sardonic suggestiveness by observing strictly the forms of simple documentation.

"Sardonic" isn't the right word: even this vulgarity is part of the subject. And since it is the fulfillment commercial America has agreed to prize, it is the fitting climax to an American affirmation:

> And there it is
> and we can't shift it or change
> it or parse it or alter it
> in any way.

Williams and the "New Mode"

by Roy Harvey Pearce

In 1922, two years after William Carlos Williams' *Kora in Hell* was published, there had come *The Waste Land* and Eliot's rise to power. Williams has again and again said what he thought about Eliot's work in comparison to his own and his hopes for it. This is the account he gives in his *Autobiography* (1951):

> Then out of the blue *The Dial* brought out *The Waste Land* and all our hilarity ended. It wiped out our world as if an atom bomb had been dropped upon it and our brave sallies into the unknown were turned to dust.
>
> To me especially it struck like a sardonic bullet. I felt at once that it had set me back twenty years, and I'm sure it did. Critically Eliot returned us to the classroom just at the moment when I felt that we were on the point of an escape to matters much closer to the essence of a new art form itself—rooted in the locality which should give it fruit. I knew at once that in certain ways I was most defeated.
>
> Eliot had turned his back on the possibility of reviving my world. And being an accomplished craftsman, better skilled in some ways than I could ever hope to be, I had to watch him carry my world off with him, the fool, to the enemy.[1]

> *Christ.* In my house there are many mansions.
> *Eliot.* I'll take the corner room on the second floor overlooking the lawns and the river. And WHO is this rabble that follows you about?
> *Christ.* Oh, some of the men I've met in my travels.
> *Eliot.* Well, if I am to follow you I'd like to know something more of your sleeping arrangements.
> *Christ.* Yes sir.

"Williams and the 'New Mode.'" Reprinted from *The Continuity of American Poetry* by Roy Harvey Pearce (Princeton, N.J.: Princeton University Press, 1961), pp. 335-48, by permission of Princeton University Press. Copyright © 1961 by Princeton University Press.

[1] *Autobiography* (New York: Random House, 1951), pp. 174-75. And see *ibid.*, p. 147; *Selected Essays* (New York: Random House, 1954), pp. 237 and 285; *Selected Letters* (New York: Ivan Obolensky, Inc., 1957), pp. 224, 226, 240. In the letter cited last (to Norman Macleod, July 25, 1945), Williams invents the following dialogue:

And he summed up thus, writing for a symposium in 1950: ". . . my own opinion of Eliot is that he was antipathetic to that which would have been required of him to be a first-rate American poet—or, rather, to write a first-rate American poem." *Focus Five: Modern American Poetry*, ed. B. Rajan (London: Dennis Dobson Ltd., 1950), p. 187.

The "our," "we," and "us" here are all aspects of the first person singular. As the lesson of *Paterson* has it, "our" world is validly "ours" only as it is "my." Williams spelled out the lesson to a correspondent in 1950:

> . . . I believe that all the old academic *values* hold today as always. Basically I am a most conventional person. But the TERMS in which we must parallel the past are entirely new and peculiar to ourselves.
> The poem to me (until I go broke) is an attempt, an experiment, a failing experiment, toward assertion with broken means but an assertion, always, of a new and total culture, the lifting of an environment to expression. Thus it is social, the poem is a social instrument—accepted or not accepted seems to be of no material importance. It embraces everything we are.[2]

How, against Eliot's claims for the power of myth and religion and Pound's for the power of "Kulchur," lift the environment into expression, and oneself with it? This was the question answered by the first four parts of *Paterson*. Moreover, *Paterson* demonstrated a means, a technique, a mode, appropriate to the poet who would carry on Whitman's work. In the letter just quoted, Williams went on to say: "Whitman to me was an instrument, one thing: he started us on the course of our researches into the nature of the line by breaking finally with English prosody. After him there has been for us no line. There will be none until we invent it. Almost everything I do is of no more interest to me than the technical addition it makes toward the discovery of a workable metric in the new mode." The new mode was a reconstitution of the old—that of Whitman and his peers—under the pressure of a kind of poetry —Eliot's—which would deny its relevance and worth.

Paterson represents only a mid-point, however climactic, in Williams' poetry. For the "line" toward which he worked came to be nothing less than the poet's means of taking absolute control over his world and of baptizing it in his own name. The strictly historical materials in *Paterson* are presented as so much *disjecta membra* and are allowed to have meaning only as they fit into the poet's scheme of things. (Which is the opposite situation to that of *The Waste*

---

[2] To Henry Wells, April 12, 1950, *Selected Letters*, p. 286. Cf. Williams' essay on *Leaves of Grass* in *Leaves of Grass: One Hundred Years After*, ed. Milton Hindus (Stanford, California: Stanford University Press, 1955), pp. 22-31.

Land.) In this poem everything must be *present;* not even in imagination can we be elsewhere than where we actually are. Yet in Williams' later poetry the historical is not present, having been eliminated altogether and restored to the process of nature from which it must have at one time been precipitated. It is the line which, as he refines it in the poems after *Paterson,* enables Williams to make such a restoration. It is also the line which brings him perilously close to the loss of his own identity. For the line of the later poems works primarily as a means of imitating the rhythms of perception and cognition, not of discriminating among and organizing what is perceived and cognized. It tends to minimize our need to separate an object perceived from its surroundings, a concept held from antecedents and consequences—as though the reality principle itself, no longer having any function, had withered away. The road away from *Paterson* has been even more dangerous than the road to it. One of the rewards in the great abundance of Williams' poetry and in the record of his compulsively public career is the perspective they give us on the affiliations of his poetry and the kind it represents with major American poetry of the nineteenth century. He has taken it upon himself to be a prophet among twentieth century American poets.

One of Williams' earliest poems, "Pastoral," describes first some sparrows which "hop ingenuously/about the pavement," then "we who are wiser/[and] shut ourselves in," and finally the old man who goes about "without looking up," yet with "tread/ . . . more majestic than/that of the Episcopal minister." In the poem Williams quite consciously risks being "insignificant" so that he can all the more powerfully say at the end: "These things/astonish me beyond words." It is that hard-earned right to say "astonish" which makes all the difference. The poem in its entirety goes thus:

> The little sparrows
> hop ingenuously
> about the pavement
> quarreling
> with sharp voices
> over those things
> that interest them.
> But we who are wiser
> shut ourselves in
> on either hand
> and no one knows

whether we think good
or evil.
        Meanwhile,
the old man who goes about
gathering dog-lime
walks in the gutter
without looking up
and his tread
is more majestic than
that of the Episcopal minister
approaching the pulpit
of a Sunday.
        These things
astonish me beyond words.

Williams' subject here is that aspect of the human condition so fascinating to the poet in the Adamic mode: the separateness of men from one another and from the things of their world. But the things are not objects for him, nor are the men *dramatis personae.* His perceptions enable him to impute to each man and each thing that he sees a vital sense of its own existence, a fateful self-consciousness; and in turn he is astonished, beyond the very words which have been his means to the imputation, with what he has discovered: Just think—there is a world like this, like me! The dividing line between what he sees and what he knows, between perception and cognition, is thus difficult to draw, except theoretically. "Astonish," as Williams uses it here, can *only* be defined by referring to the things which draw the word out from him. This is precisely the effect that Williams wants. His so-called "naturalism," his fascination with the "anti-poetic" (which his friend Stevens early pointed out[3]) derives from a compulsion to define separateness (or alienation) in terms of the insignificant (or "anti-poetic").

In "Pastoral" the simple, separate things upon which the imagination feeds have an integrity and vitality so marked as to convince the poet that he cannot relate them coherently one to another. He cannot quite "understand" the world in which he lives.

[3] Preface to Williams' *Collected Poems, 1921-1931* (New York, 1934), as reprinted in *Opus Posthumous,* ed. S. F. Morse (New York: Alfred A. Knopf, Inc., 1957), pp. 254-57. Stevens accordingly characterized Williams as a "romantic" poet—and I think, if his use of that confusing term is rightly understood, quite properly. Miss Vivienne Koch's New Critical rejection of Stevens' characterization is, I conclude, beside the point, because she, put on her guard by the very sound of the word, misses the point. See her *William Carlos Williams* (Norfolk, Conn.: New Directions Publishing Corporation, 1950), pp. 60-62.

He can *almost* understand it, and accordingly is quite willing to
point up his predicament with appropriate pathos and sentimen-
talism:

> so much depends
> upon
>
> a red wheel
> barrow
>
> glazed with rain
> water
>
> beside the white
> chickens.

In this notably sentimental piece (XXI of *Spring and All*), Wil-
liams can only dimly specify "what" depends—himself in his voca-
tion as poet. He assures himself that he is what he is by virtue of
his power to collocate such objects into sharply annotated images
like these. He must feel himself into the things of his world; for he
is dependent on them as occasions to be himself—as poet. Perhaps
—and herein lies the pathos—they depend on him as much as he
depends on them. "So much depends" too upon a poet's being there
to make them what, at their best, they can be: objects in a poem.
At its worst this is togetherness in a chicken-yard. At its best it is
an exercise in the creation of the poetic out of the anti-poetic. Not
the least significant characteristic of Williams' work is that the
best in it cannot but bring out the worst. Like his friend and enemy
Pound, he has had the courage to go all the way with his convic-
tions.

Some of the poems before *Paterson*—so many as to form a defin-
able group and to evince a "theme"—are about persons, quite often
the person of the poet. "Danse Russe" for example:

> If I when my wife is sleeping
> and the baby and Kathleen
> are sleeping
> and the sun is a flame-white disc
> in silken mists
> above shining trees,—
> if I in my north room
> dance naked, grotesquely
> before my mirror
> waving my shirt round my head

and singing softly to myself:
"I am lonely, lonely.
I was born to be lonely,
I am best so!"
If I admire my arms, my face,
my shoulders, flanks, buttocks
against the yellow drawn shades,—

Who shall say I am not
the happy genius of my household?

Poems like "Danse Russe" are essentially "talking" poems. Other examples are "Smell!," "Impromptu: The Suckers," "Death," and "The Widow's Lament in Springtime," which begins marvelously:

Sorrow is my own yard
where the new grass
flames as it has flamed
often before but not
with the cold fire
that closes round me this year.

In such a poem the speaker is made quite self-consciously to ask what he is doing in our world. If the poem works, what is for him a question is for us an answer. The difference between this sort of poem and the traditional dramatic monologue is that whereas in the latter the speaker is talking to us, in the former he is talking to himself. Talking becomes a necessary means not so much of communicating as of creating one's sense of one's self.

And there are the poems primarily of "seeing." Here is the most famous example, the first poem from the group called "Spring and All":

By the road to the contagious hospital
under the surge of the blue
mottled clouds driven from the
northeast—a cold wind. Beyond, the
waste of broad, muddy fields
brown with dried weeds, standing and fallen

patches of standing water
the scattering of tall trees

All along the road the reddish
purplish, forked, upstanding, twiggy
stuff of bushes and small trees

with dead, brown leaves under them
leafless vines—

Lifeless in appearance, sluggish
dazed spring approaches—

They enter the new world naked,
cold, uncertain of all
save that they enter. All about them
the cold, familiar wind—

Now the grass, tomorrow
the stiff curl of wildcarrot leaf
One by one objects are defined—
It quickens: clarity, outline of leaf

But now the stark dignity of
entrance—Still, the profound change
has come upon them: rooted, they
grip down and begin to awaken.

Here (other examples are "Spring Strains," "Queen-Ann's-Lace," "Young Sycamore," and "Nantucket") the procedure is to discover "things" and to view what has been discovered sharply and precisely and separately; yet at the same time (since the seeing is a continuous process) through the creative force of the seeing, to realize the paradox of continuity in change, relatedness in non-relatedness. In the poem I have just quoted a perception of a series of objects is made to blend into a thought ("It quickens:"), so that it *is* the thought. The implicit claim is not that one sees objects and then expresses their meaning, but rather that they are there, ready to express themselves for one's seeing. The poet *sees* their meaning, as he *hears* the meaning of those who populate his "talking" poems. His role as poet is to recognize, by a kind of affinity, their vital principle and to find the words whereby it might be expressed.

No ideas but in things, as Williams says in *Paterson*—where, writing in both modes at once, he most fully realizes the possibilities of his kind of poem. This is what he called "the new mode." The role of the "line" here is to control and modulate revelation according to the nature and needs of poet and reader, and of the language they share. Both precision of speech and sharpness of vision are subordinated to the movement toward that awareness which is for the poet antecedent to them—their occasion, in fact. Yet we can disinguish between that of which we become aware and ourselves in the act of becoming aware. Mediating between us and the world of the poem,

between subject and object, is the poem itself. This should be
enough.

Yet Williams has come to want more than this. He would have
the poem be the means whereby subject and object are fused. To-
ward this purpose he has directed the bulk of his poems since
Paterson. He was, in fact, moving toward it at the time he was
working on *Paterson.* There is "Choral: The Pink Church," in
which we read:

> Sing!
> transparent to the light
>   through which the light
> shines, through the stone,
>   until
> the stone-light glows,
>   pink jade
> —that is the light and is
>   a stone
> and is a church—if the image
>   hold . . .

"The Pink Church" is the poet's world, and all the persons, places,
and things it contains; much of the poem runs, Whitmanlike, over
their names, so attempting to absorb them into that ultimate pink-
ness, that ultimate light, that ultimate revelation, into which a full
sense of their presence must issue. Likewise, there is "Burning the
Christmas Greens," which begins:

> Their time past, pulled down
> cracked and flung to the fire
> —go up in a roar
>
> All recognition lost, burnt clean
> clean in the flame, the green
> dispersed, a living red,
> flame red, red as blood wakes
> on the ash—

Again, that light which moves as the blood moves. The theme of
the poem is put explicitly toward the end:

>   . . . Transformed!
>
> Violence leaped and appeared.
> Recreant! roared to life

as the flame rose through and
our eyes recoiled from it.

The poem is intended to manifest a resurrection—all the more
marvellous because it is made up of words, which are death. "The
Pink Church" is nominally what I have called a "talking" poem;
"Burning the Christmas Greens" is nominally a seeing poem. Yet
how easily, for Williams, the one becomes the other! How easily
that creative awareness toward which they lead becomes ritual! How
naturally it takes its substance from matters associated traditionally
with ritual—churches and Christmas greens! The poem has become
a prayer; but he who prays, prays only to himself and that part of
himself he can discover in his world.

Because Williams has wanted so much from poetry, he has pro-
claimed from the rooftops of the world the necessity of reconceiving
its technique. Technique has meant for him only the "line" and a
"workable metric"—as though the sole necessary condition for a
poem were an adequate prosody. In the poems from which I have
just quoted the incantatory overrides logic, structure, and the dis-
position of meaning. The millennialist expectation is that out of
poems written in this "new mode" there will come a "new lan-
guage." "The measurement of the poetic line of the future," he
wrote in 1955, "has to be expanded so as to take a larger grip of its
material." Pound had almost seen this, Williams declared, but not
quite. And he continued:

> The grammar of the term, variable foot, is simply what it describes
> itself to be: a poetic foot that is not fixed but varies with the de-
> mands of the language, keeping the measured emphasis as it may oc-
> cur in the line. Its characteristic, where it differs from the fixed foot
> with which we are familiar, is that it ignores the counting of the num-
> ber of syllables in the line, which is the mark of the usual scansion,
> for a measure of the ear, a more sensory counting. . . .
> The advantage of the practice over the old mode of measuring is
> that without inversion it permits the poet to use the language he nat-
> urally speaks, provided he has it well under control and does not lose
> the measured order of the words.

Behind this theorizing about prosody, there lies the mystique of
the new mode:

> The only measured form of language . . . is its poetry. Therefore
> ineffective as it may appear to be as a weapon, in the public eye, it
> is only by attacking there, . . . that our actions can have a lasting
> effect.

On that basis alone will a new language, let us presume it to be the American language, be fit to trust its organization.[4]

Again: Joel Barlow's hopes for a universal language, at base presumably American. "Without measure, we are lost," Williams had written in 1954.[5] In this radically alternative version of the theory of Eliot's "Music of Poetry," man is the measure of all things; but the essence of man, and thus the ground of the measure, is expressed not in what he has done or what he is doing, but rather in the way his language bids him do it. The theory of the variable foot is simple—just as a magical formula is simple when compared to the wonders it will work. To be true it *has* to be simple. Like Eliot's theory, Williams' looks toward its own kind of mirage, beyond mere language. Yielding to the demands of language, the poet yields to that which is essential in his sense of himself in his world. This is the extreme formulation of the "new mode," in which, as Wallace Stevens was to say, "the poem is the cry of its occasion." At its best—in the first four parts of *Paterson*, above all—the new mode is Williams' means, in a phrase from "A Sort of a Song," "through metaphor to reconcile/the people and the stones."

"Reconcile" is the key term. Reconciliation requires a balance between people and stones, with the poem as fulcrum, which after the first four parts of *Paterson* Williams has more and more disclaimed. In his later poetry the measure-as-movement has increasingly come to override the measure-as-gauge. The variety of the foot tends to refer back to the potentiality for variety in the poet, not in his relations with his world. Explicitly rejecting an orthodox Christian world, "a woman's world,/of crossed sticks, stopping/thought," he decides that "A new world/is only a new mind" ("To Daphne and Virginia"). The mind is the poet's, its activity "invention" (a word of which, since *Paterson*, he has grown increasingly fond) according to the principles of the "measured form of language."

This is part of the end of his long "Asphodel, that Greeny Flower" (1955):

[4] "The American Language—Again," *Pound Newsletter,* No. 8 (October 1955), pp. 2-7. See also *I Wanted to Write a Poem* (Boston: Beacon Press, 1958), p. 82.
[5] "On Measure," *Selected Essays* (New York: Random House, 1954), p. 340. First published in *Origin* (Spring 1954), 194-99. See also "The American Idiom," *Between Worlds,* No 2 (1961), pp. 234-35; and Walter Sutton, "A Visit with William Carlos Williams," *Minnesota Review,* I (Spring 1961), pp. 309-24. In these recent essays Williams speaks even more like Barlow in *The Columbiad;* for he insists that the "variable foot"—used in a line shorter than Whitman's—involves our new notions of time and space, man and matter, and so is above all "modern."

Only the imagination is real!
          I have declared it
                    time without end.
If a man die
          it is because death
                    has first
possessed his imagination.
          But if he refuse death—
                    no greater evil
can befall him
          unless it be the death of love
                    meet him
in full career.
          Then indeed
                    for him
the light has gone out.
But love and the imagination
          are of a piece,
                    swift as the light
To avoid destruction.
          So we come to watch time's flight
                    as we might watch
summer lightning
          or fireflies, secure,
                    by grace of the imagination,
safe in its care.
          For if
                    the light itself
has escaped,
          the whole edifice opposed to it
                    goes down.
Light, the imagination
          and love,
                    in our age,
by natural law,
          which we worship,
                    maintain
all of a piece
          their dominance.

Here Williams must turn for his image, as have so many poets
before him, to the all-suffusing force of light. Elsewhere in the poem,
against the Eliot of the *Quartets* and the Pound of the *Rock-Drill*

Cantos, he challenges Dante and the whole history of Christian belief. He declares that the true light is an inner one which only the poet, his verses vibrating with his own radiance, can turn on the world—and can then, and only then, receive as a blessing from his world. As he conceives of himself in this poem, he is no longer alienated; yet he has no home to go to, nor has he undone his alienation by making a home for himself. For he, or so he would convince us, has been home all the time; and he has been alienated not from the world, but from himself, which is all the world he has. Brave new world, the movement of his verses lead him to say, that has me in it!

The world of *Paterson* was full of a number of things. Knowing this, the poet could love his world. The world of the "Asphodel" poem, and of other poems like it, is full of one thing, the poet. Knowing this, who can the poet love but himself—or all those whom he can metamorphose into an aspect, or a function, of himself? Thus the physician, having spent a long life healing others, now finally heals himself. Adam—the Adam of the contagious hospital, of the world that is *Paterson*—magicks himself into believing that he has never left Eden. He has just imagined that he has. Now he can imagine that he has not.

So in 1958 Williams put a coda to *Paterson. Paterson Five* is not, I think, really meant to continue and develop the motifs of the rest of the poem. *Paterson Five* is a poem about the making of *Paterson One-Four.* The poet is now an old man, sure that his has been the right way, that through love for his world (it is both "virgin and whore") a poet may save it from the past for which it yearns and the future which it fears. Only "the world/of the imagination . . . endures." He sees everything—people, works of arts, objects of nature—as being nothing if he cannot bring them alive now, and himself as nothing if he cannot help bring them alive. Moreover, he has no need to look into the future, the prophet being just the historian turned backwards. He knows what he wants:

> Not prophecy! NOT prophecy!
> but the thing itself!

But he *is* a prophet: one who can fuse past and future into present. As in *Paterson Three,* he quotes a letter from Pound expounding his cracker-barrel economics in his cracker-barrel style; but this time Williams puts over against it not geological statistics (essential anti-poetry) but a section that begins:

There is a woman in our town
walks rapidly, flat bellied
in worn slacks upon the street
where I saw her.

—a single instance of the poet's all-pervading life instinct and his belief in the authenticity of his ever-contemporaneous world and himself in it, creator of all he surveys. But he is now an old man, meditating in painfully sharp detail the passions of others. He figures himself (as he calls to mind a medieval tapestry and considers the passion of its maker) as a wounded unicorn—"I Paterson, the King-self"—inevitably betrayed by his virgin-whore. Yet

                       The Unicorn
has no match
          or mate . the artist
               has no peer .

He even quotes from a television interview in which he had defined poetry: "A poem is a complete little universe. It exists separately. Any poem that has worth expresses the whole life of the poet. It gives a view of what the poet is." Not what the world is, or could be, or should be, but what the poet is. His procreant urge stays with him; his powers lessen. In all honesty he can only say to himself, "Paterson,/keep your pecker up/whatever the detail!"

This is the fifth act of a *Tempest* not properly anticipated in the first four. *Paterson Five* lacks one of the primary qualities of the four sections which precede it: a fecundating sense of the place and its inhabitants. "Anywhere is everywhere," Williams decides. He has pushed his line to a point where it has become a means of treating persons and places solely as aspects of himself. The thing itself turns out to be Williams' thing and no one else's. The difference is between two meanings of "thing itself": thing in *it*self; and thing in *my*self. *Paterson Five* is an incantatory poem, the Adamic poet's unmediated vision. The act of the poem has as its end not to discover or invent the world but to celebrate the power of invention itself. Thus the ending:

The measure intervenes, to measure is all we know,

       a choice among the measures . .

            the measured dance

"unless the scent of a rose
                    startle us anew"

Equally laughable
                    is to assume to know nothing, a
                                        chess game
massively, "materially", compounded!

                    Yo ho! ta ho!

We know nothing and can know nothing   .
                         but
the dance, to dance to a measure
contrapuntally,
                    Satyrically, the tragic foot.

The counterpoint, however, counterpoints only itself.

On *Paterson*, Book One

by Sister M. Bernetta Quinn

Few poems have ever been priced as high as William Carlos
Williams's *Paterson*, if one may borrow the central metaphor of the
third book in order to suggest the enormous cost in concentration
which must be met before any adequate evaluation can be made.
If this work were built around a consistently presented hero—the
Paterson of the title—that cost might not be so prohibitive as many
readers will find it; but when Williams asserts in the introduction
to Book Three ("The Library") that Paterson is not only the hero
but also the heroine, not only a city but also cliffs and a waterfall,
one cries out for a critic to assist him, as the sea-god did Peleus, in
conquering the metamorphic problem. Before judging the total
merit of *Paterson*, however, one must weather a preliminary season
of understanding, of looking hard and often at aim and structure—
in brief, of giving the poem the creative reading that such an under-
taking deserves. The poet, realizing the difficulty of meeting this
high cost, has given some measure of help in the headnote to the
entire poem, and also in the list of topics which he places imme-
diately after the words "Book One," as if in apposition; the latter
consists of eighteen phrases separated by semicolons, each phrase a
possible definition of *Paterson*. The last of these phrases is "a dis-
persal and a metamorphosis."

This metamorphic emphasis is particularly prominent in the
methods Williams uses to interchange man and certain aspects of
his environment in order to compel a new awareness in citizens of
the Waste Land:

> Truthfully pleading his inability to handle traditional coin tradition-
> ally, Williams improvises, issues a fluid currency of his own; in *Pater-*

son, a set of protean, imagist-symbolist centers of force which polarize
his loose, fragmentary material.[1]

Like Hart Crane, he has searched the world about him for a focal
symbol, hitting upon one even more fitted to his poetic intentions
than was Brooklyn Bridge to Crane's. He has seen in Paterson, New
Jersey, neighbor to his own Rutherford, a point suitable for the
intersection of several themes obsessing the modern artist. The very
name, Paterson, with its Latin and Germanic components, unites
the generating principle with the result of generation: man is both
subject and object in the design of reality, since through perception,
according to Williams, he creates what lies about him. In the Preface
to the poem Williams, echoing Eliot, says paradoxically: "For the
beginning is assuredly/the end—since we know nothing, pure/and
simple, beyond/our own complexities." If Wordsworth's child was
father to the man, Williams' father is also son. When considered
as combining Latin and French roots, *Paterson* may also imply the
father of sound; again, its connotations include the homonym of
son (sun):

> It [Paterson] is the ignorant sun
> rising in the slot of
> hollow suns risen, so that never in this
> world will a man live well in his body
> save dying. . . .

But the significance of Paterson as locale is far more than verbal,
as Williams reveals in the first book, "The Delineaments of the
Giants."

In establishing the elemental character of the place, the poet de-
scribes two titanic figures: masculine (Paterson the city) and femi-
nine (Garrett Mountain). The first lies on his right side, sleeping
on the bank of the Passaic River, head near the Great Falls, facing
the woman, who is also asleep. Only the dreams of Paterson are
stirring; they walk about the city as its citizens—unaware of the
mighty mind which is their source and hence unable to realize their
destinies. Of all American cities Paterson was indeed an excellent
choice for such a concept, with its falls which Hamilton hoped
would furnish water power enough to supply manufactured goods
for the whole country, falls which even today make it the largest
single silk-producing center in the United States. Besides, close to
the coast, it is connected with the sea by the Passaic River and with

[1] R. W. Flint, " 'I Will Teach You My Townspeople,' " *The Kenyon Review,*
XII (Autumn 1950), 538.

inland waterways by canal, two facts making it desirable for the elucidation of Williams' "dispersal" motif, referred to in the head-note.

The setting for this drama of giants is given in a spirit of local pride. Largely through prose links, Williams as the poem progresses sketches in several places which any good map of the district will render easy to visualize: Notch Brook, the Valley of the Rocks, Ramapos Valley, Pompton, New Barbadoes Neck, Manchester, Singac, Morris Mountain, Hohokus, the Goffle. Williams feels very keenly about place, a concept which anchors his philosophy of "no ideas but in things." He disagrees with Eliot's rather glib assertion in the *Quartets* that place is only place, and that what is actual is actual only for one place. On the contrary, he believes that only in some one place does the universal ever become actual, and that therefore place is the only universal. He has been criticized for living out his lifetime in one fairly small city of a small Eastern state. Williams gives his apologia in these words:

> We live only in one place at a time but far from being bound by it, only through it do we realize our freedom. Place then ceases to be a restriction, we do not have to abandon our familiar and known to achieve distinction but far from constricting ourselves, not searching for some release in some particular place, rather in that place, if we only make ourselves sufficiently aware of it, do join with others in other places.[2]

Paterson, however, is his supreme apologia. In view of Williams's cardinal principle (no ideas but in things) one can see how tremendously important setting is for his purposes. Paterson's ideas, his thoughts, are all things, such as the "blank faces of houses" or "cylindrical trees." The inhabitants, ignorant of the forces motivating them, are thoughts that are also things, a "thousand automatons."

Williams throughout his poem has given the city a life organic as a man's life. In the prose passages he has taken actual names and places in order to ground the experiment in actuality. It is a matter of record that the Revolutionary period considered the Falls a "wonder" along with other freaks of nature such as Peter Van Winkle, the dwarf; that sturgeon as large as that described in Book One were formerly caught in the Passaic; that Cornelius Doremus left an estate of $419.58½; that Paterson had a noted German Singing Society; that Dean William McNulty of Saint Joseph's Catholic Church was a greatly admired leader in the city; that Jack Reed,

Bill Haywood, and "Gurley" Flynn helped in the 1913 I.W.W. strike, in connection with which the Paterson Pageant was staged in Madison Square Garden; that William Kieft, Governor General of New Amsterdam, persecuted the Indians in 1643; that three weeks after the big fire of February 1902 the worst of four bad floods ravaged Paterson, with a tornado occurring the same year; that the Van Giesens and the Van Houtens were prominent among early Paterson families. But Williams does not always feel bound to conform to the precise details of history; for instance, the tornado of 1902 is given as preceding the fire and flood though actually it was several months later.

In several instances, Williams' prose links dealing with Paterson's past are not original at all but are merely taken verbatim from William Nelson's *History of the City of Paterson and the County of Passaic*.[3] Examples are the description of an Indian sacrifice ceremony (37, 38); the artesian-well passage (11); Peter Van Winkle, the dwarf (100); the Van Giesen witch story (269); the Hopper incident (345, 346). Since this mosaic technique has been used five times in the poem, it is probable that thorough going research in libraries of the region would yield the sources for other historical interludes. The famous Dutch lullaby used in *Paterson* is quoted in the history of Paterson by Nelson and Shriner,[4] which also gives an account of the Garrett Mountain riot of 1880, in which John J. Van Houten was killed (II, 499, 500), an account which opens with the same words as the one in *Paterson*.

Some readers have grown impatient with these prose insertions, failing to see the reasons for their inclusion other than as contrast or as illustrations of the breakdown of language. Perhaps they can best be understood as a study in sources, an ignorance of which is one of the main causes why citizens of Paterson walk around asleep, desires locked in their minds, inarticulate. Williams has earlier condemned his countrymen for not knowing their roots, from which their bones, thought, and action have sprung. (*In the American Grain*, 113.) Among these sources are the Puritans, represented in the poem by the witch-hunting Merselis Van Giesen; Revolutionary politicians such as Hamilton; Indians, to whom five different episodes are devoted; Negroes, both West Indian and American-born, such as D. J. B. in Book Three; Irish (McGuckin), German (Spangermacher), Dutch (Kieft, Van Houten), Scandinavian (Ferguson),

---

[3] (Paterson, New Jersey: The Press Printing and Publishing Company, 1901).
[4] William Nelson and Charles A. Shriner, *History of Paterson and Its Environs*, (3 vols.; New York and Chicago: Lewis Historical Publishing Company, 1920), I, 156.

French (Jan de la Montagne), English (Lambert). Special attention
is called to Paterson's heterogeneous population in "The Delinea-
ments of the Giants" by a listing of 1870 statistics: native-born,
20,711; French, 237; German, 1,420; English, 3,343; Irish, 5,124;
Scotch, 879; Hollanders, 1,360; Swiss, 170. It is no wonder that in
June of each year Paterson holds a Festival of Nations. Some prose
links are harder to justify as sources, as biography of a region, than
others are; for example, it is difficult to see just how the thumbnail
sketch of "Billy" (Book One) or the anecdote about the dog Musty
(Book Two) fits into the design, except as "modern replicas," de-
generations of a worthier past. It is safe, however, to assume that
they are not irrelevancies. One way of regarding them might be as
manifestations of the irrational, so large a part of every life though
impregnable to explication.

By returning to the sources of Paterson as city, Williams means
to explain, in terms of a traditional microcosm–macrocosm analogy,
the intricacies of twentieth century Paterson as man, who differs
from Oliver in Santayana's novel, *The Last Puritan,* a paragraph
from which forms the headnote to Book Three:

> Cities, for Oliver, were not a part of nature. He could hardly
> feel, he could hardly admit even when it was pointed out to him,
> that cities are a second body for the human mind, a second organism,
> more rational, permanent and decorative than the animal organism
> of flesh and bone: a work of natural yet moral art, where the soul
> sets up her trophies of action and instruments of pleasure.

Williams feels, not only that the mind animates Paterson the city,
but that the city contains within it the life of any individual citizen,
concretized, since a man is what he experiences. This metaphor is
pushed even further in Book Four, with the earth itself becoming a
macrocosm of the human Paterson and including both sexes:

> Woman is the weaker vessel, but
> the mind is neutral, a bead linking
> continents, brow and toe

The Passaic River is used in the poem to represent the giant
Paterson's stream of consciousness; this requires a leap from the
city where the citizen-dreams walk about to the place where the
river "crashes from the edge of the gorge/in a recoil of spray and
rainbow mists—." The parallel between the currents of the Passaic
and Paterson's thoughts (their interlacing, repulsion, advance, ed-
dying, coalescence, leap and fall, retaking of the course) is worked
out with a clarity of invention that brings the vehicle of the meta-

phor sharply before the eyes and into the ears in the best objectivist manner. A subsidiary meaning concerns the river as a figure of the seminal fluid: ("The multiple seed,/packed tight with detail, soured,/is lost in the flux. . . .") Love between man and woman must beget marriage, not death, as in the old plays—but how can it when divorce, not union, is the sign of the times? "Divorce is/the sign of knowledge in our time,/divorce! divorce!"

Louis Martz, reviewing *Paterson One* and *Two,* explains the river's import thus:

> The basic image of Book I was the Passaic River, metamorphosed into a symbol of the flow of all human mind, including the mind's half-conscious sense of powers beyond itself; the falls of the Passaic seemed to represent the power of the poet to interrupt, refract, and coalesce this flow into a quivering and terrifying scene of beauty.[5]

Such an interpretation assumes that the problem which Williams poses reaches solution, but is it so solved in the poem itself? Allied to Martz's view, yet distinct from it and perhaps more accurate, is the view based on still another level of reference, the identification of the waterfall with language, a language not understood or at best misunderstood, which drives Paterson to shaken intensity as he tries to comprehend its cataract. The unheeded harangue of the Evangelist in Book Two is called a falls; often the Passaic is termed a voice. None but the poet can furnish the lexicon whereby this torrent may become meaningful, and no poet has come—at least, no poet able to comb out the language that pours from the rafter of a rock's lip. Yet one further stratum of the Falls image is its designation, at the end of the third book, as the present connecting the past and future:

> The past above, the future below
> and the present pouring down: the roar,
> the roar of the present, a speech—
> is, of necessity, my sole concern .

Williams is alert to every possibility of his pivotal metaphor, water, in illustrating the metamorphosis announced in his headnote. From time to time he adverts to the various phases water undergoes: the process of evaporation by which it is "lifted as air"; its polychromatic glory as a rainbow (a phenomenon particularly impressive at the Falls, in the season of melting snows or heavy rains); reduction to waterdrops again, when it is "divided as the dew"; "the

[5] "Recent Poetry," *The Yale Review,* XXXVIII (Autumn 1948), 149.

clouds resolved into a sandy sluice"; "floating mists, to be rained
down and /regathered into a river that flows/and encircles." He sees
it as "clear ice," as the ice-cake in which Sam Patch, the daredevil
jumper, was frozen after the fatal plunge into the Genesee River
at Rochester. He uses the parable of the sower to show how crystals
of snow can be wasted, lost in the flux:

> the snow falling into the water,
> part upon the rock, part in the dry weeds
> and part into the water where it
> vanishes—its form no longer what it was:

And he pictures in remarkably vivid detail the effects of the flood
after the winter's snow has metamorphosed into trickling rivulets
which gather for destruction.

A prose item about David Hower's 1857 discovery of pearls in
the mussels of Notch Brook separates the initial appearance of
Paterson as giant from his first metamorphosis: a conversion into
Mr. Paterson the poet, whose "works/have been done into French/
and Portuguese." He has gone away to rest and write, leaving his
thoughts to sit and stand in the city bus, to alight and scatter.
Immediately after equating the poet Paterson's thoughts with the
citizens, Williams shifts in protean fashion to "the regularly ordered
plateglass of/his thoughts," again fusing the subject and object—
the reflected is also the reflector. He underscores the unifying char-
acter of the metaphor by using, at the conclusion of the stanza, the
singular noun *thought:* "his thought is listed in the Telephone/
Directory." At this point the pronoun *I* is introduced as distinct
from Paterson, evidently only one of the ideas mirrored in his
thoughts; such a technique is bound to result in confusion for the
reader unless he can preserve extreme agility in the following of
images.

Set up as a complement of the city–man Paterson, the mountain–
woman symbol changes throughout the work in equally protean
manner. In Book One she lies:

> facing him, his
> arm supporting her, by the *Valley of the Rocks,* asleep.
> Pearls at her ankles, her monstrous hair
> spangled with apple-blossoms is scattered about into
> the back country. . . .

The Park is her head, the features of which have been carved by
the Passaic out of the colored rocks. A few pages later this image
is blended with that of a flower to which Williams has previously

in the poem compared the woman. But no bee carries fertilizing pollen to the heart of this flower; instead it sinks back into the ground, wilting, disappearing, destined for sterility instead of fruitful marriage. This desecration of the feminine principle is emphasized in the prose link immediately following, an account of how Jackson sold English girls and West Indian Negresses during the American Revolution, and of how Cromwell shipped thousands of Irish women to the Barbadoes for the slave market.

Next, the mountain–flower–woman becomes the first wife of an African chief (photographed for the *National Geographic* with her eight successors), scowling, worn out, yet elemental as a tree trunk from which the other wives grow like branches, a parallel of the tree metaphor used for Paterson himself in Book Two. The various semantic threads are twisted tightly together (flower, rock, and wife united) as Williams elucidates his symbolism:

> Which is to say, though it be poorly
> said, there is a first wife
> and a first beauty, complex, ovate—
> the woody sepals standing back under
> the stress to hold it there, innate
>
> a flower within a flower whose history
> (within the mind) crouching
> among the ferny rocks, laughs at the names
> by which they think to trap it.

The first section of Book One (each of the four large divisions of the poem is broken up into three parts) finishes with a prose link developing the third metamorphosis: N. F. Paterson, the old time Jersey Patriot, otherwise known as Sam Patch (c. 1807–1829), who astonished crowds all over America by diving from "cliffs and masts, rocks and bridges." Williams explains that the initials N. F. stand for Noah (the Biblical victor over water) and Faitoute ("Some things can be done as well as others"), the latter a name which Paterson is to assume intermittently for the rest of the poem, its sense suggesting action in opposition to the passive nature of his feminine partner. *The Dictionary of American Biography* relates how Sam "in his cups would parrot his two apothegms: 'There's no mistake in Sam Patch' and 'Some things can be done as well as others.' " He is finally overcome by the failure of language, falling sideways in his 125-foot leap into the falls of the Genesee River to hit the water and disappear until the breaking up of the ice the following spring. It is interesting to note that the plunge took place on Friday the thirteenth.

Williams does not tell us what Patch said in the inadequate little speech which preceded his jump, but Jenny Marsh Parker has preserved it in her history of Rochester:

Napoleon was a great man and a great general. He conquered armies and he conquered nations. But he couldn't jump the Genesee Falls. Wellington was a great man and a great soldier. He conquered armies and he conquered nations, and he conquered Napoleon, but he couldn't jump the Genesee Falls. That was left for me to do, and I can do it, and will! [6]

Enormous interest and a strangely high emotional pitch of public recrimination surrounded the Patch incident, including a persistent expectation of his "resurrection," an interest recorded in the plays and poems on his fate written soon after the disaster. Even in his own day the victim was a symbol, as he is in *Paterson;* the fact that his death occurred not at the Passaic but at the Genesee Falls, a region where he was cut off from his sources, is of special symbolic importance, and the name of the Falls with its resemblance to *genesis* ironic.

To universalize his statement, Williams introduces Mrs. Hopper Cumming as a complement for Sam Patch; Mrs. Cumming, bride of a few months, mysteriously falls to her death from the cliff, in what is perhaps as intentional a plunge as Patch's professional jumps. William Nelson, the standard historian of the Paterson region, calls this the "most romantically tragic incident in the history of the Passaic Falls." William Carlos Williams gives the story in florid, sentimental, overwritten prose.

But Williams' style is conservative when compared to some of the contemporary versions. One Peter Archdeacon, prominent Paterson citizen, after telling of a blackbird which, like a supernatural warning, hovered around the Reverend Mr. Cumming's head during his sermon on Sunday, June 21, 1812, concludes his eulogy of the minister and his wife thus: "The next day alas! before the sun had veiled his head beyond yon western hill, the flush was nipped, and the lovely seraph's spirit fled to the regions of the blessed!" [7]

---

[6] *Rochester: A Story Historical* (Rochester, New York: Scrantom, Wetmore and Company, 1884), p. 188.

[7] William Nelson, *History of the Old Dutch Church at Totowa, Paterson, New Jersey, 1755-1827* (Paterson, New Jersey: The Press Printing and Publishing Company, 1892), p. 40.

The language ("Stale as a whale's breath") in the relation of the tragedy, both in this account and in *Paterson,* indicates how wide the chasm between words and events has become. Since Mrs. Cumming had been standing twenty feet from the edge for half an hour or more, her fall is inexplicable other than as a result of the magnetic power of the waters roaring down in their untranslatable beauty or as an escape from a life in which falsity has superseded the truth of ideas located in things. One senses that Williams does not consider the drowning accidental, from these lines in Book Two: "leaped (or fell) without a/language, tongue-tied/the language worn out."

After the story of Patch, Williams shifts his central personality back to the sleeping giant:

> with the roar of the river
> forever in our ears (arrears)
> inducing sleep and silence, the roar
> of eternal sleep . . challenging
> our waking—

With the thunder of the Passaic in his ears, he dreams of the "I" in whom he has, after all, no real interest. That *I,* however, goes on speculating, considering how "the ground has undergone/a subtle transformation, its identity altered" since the days of the Indians. The problem, he muses, is to interrelate details on the new ground, a difficult task possible only if the disparate can be pulled together "to clarify/and compress"; an assonance must be set up, a homologue. One of Williams' ways of doing this has been referred to by Vivienne Koch (in her book on the poet) as an echo device, a practice different from the tissue of repetitions which gives *Paterson* its orchestral quality.[8] Over a hundred times he juxtaposes identical words or phrases, enriching the musical development (as Randall Jarrell has strikingly pointed out in his *Partisan Review* comments on the red bird's song[9]), suggesting the echo usually connected with the scene of a waterfall, even hinting at the narcissistic theory which the very word *Paterson* crystallizes, perhaps also paralleling that stutter which is descriptive of contemporary effort to use the language.

Replacing the third person singular with *you,* Williams in Book One, section two, separates the giants from their human replicas as

---

[8] *William Carlos Williams* (Norfolk, Conn.: New Directions Publishing Corporation, 1950), p. 126.

[9] "The Poet and His Public," *Partisan Review,* XIII (September-October 1946), 494.

he writes of a conversation between two lovers, against the back-
ground of the Falls. The couple is isolated in the stream of Fai-
toute's thoughts. Then, at the beginning of the next section, he
nimbly turns the symbol of woman back into a flower, stressing
again the permanence of art, which will outlast the artist.

He starts by alluding to woman in her character of rose carved
out of the red rock, destined to remain after that nine-months'
wonder, Paterson the man, or even the city itself, has vanished:

> So you think because the rose
> is red that you shall have the mastery?
> The rose is green and will bloom,
> overtopping you, green, livid
> green when you shall no more speak, or
> taste, or even be.

But whatever the future triumph of the rock, its present is a deg-
radation, daily raped as it is by the "greast beast." Paterson sees
this debasement; he broods over the woman's fate: "What can he
think else—along/the gravel of the ravished park, torn by/the wild
workers' children tearing up the grass,/kicking, screaming." Just as
the university has corrupted the language ("knowledgeable idiots"
blocking genuine communication) so have the dyeworks corrupted
the river into which their waste products are spewed; since man
and the city are one, an interpenetration, what defiles the mind of
one defiles the other. Miss Koch calls this section of the poem "a
powerful attack on 'learning' in which the persistent change and
metamorphosis of natural forms is used as counterfoil to 'the whole
din of fracturing thought.' " [10]

Moreover, man's bride, the imagination, figured by the Park,
cannot avoid this corruption. In commenting on Shapiro's *Essay
on Rime,* Williams has used the analogy of a composite woman as
representing rime; he says: "We express ourselves there (men) as
we might on the whole body of the various female could we ever
gain access to her (which we cannot and never shall)." Yet we should
not, he goes on, feel thwarted as artists, since "We do the best we
can—as much as the females of our souls permit." [11] We cannot at-
tain the composite woman, but there are always two women, three
women, "Innumerable women, each like a flower," though "only
one man—like a city." Throughout the course of the whole poem
these representative women appear, "each like a flower." One is

[10] *William Carlos Williams,* pp. 128, 129.
[11] "Shapiro Is All Right," *The Kenyon Review,* VIII (Winter 1946), 123.

reminded of Thomas Hardy's search for the ideal woman in *The
Well-Beloved*. Paterson's problem, as he finally summarizes it in
Book Four is:

> To bring himself in,
> hold together wives in one wife and
> at the same time scatter it,
> the one in all of them   .

Another meaning of this composite female is society itself, apart
from which the poet cannot write immortally or even validly, since
he needs the nourishment which she alone can give him. This is a
Whitmanesque idea, denied on one hand by Pound and apostoli-
cally affirmed on the other by Williams, with poor Hart Crane in
the middle, torn between the extremes as he struggled to build his
Bridge. Williams has made the identification of woman and society
explicit in a letter to an Australian editor; speaking of the poet,
he says:

> He will continue to produce only if his attachments to society con-
> tinue adequate. If a man in his fatuous dreams cuts himself off from
> that supplying female, he dries up his sources—as Pound did in the
> end heading straight for literary sterility.[12]

The poet's function, then, becomes a metamorphic one:

> Let me insist, the poet's very life, but also his forms originate in the
> political, social and economic maelstrom on which he rides. At his
> best he transmutes them to new values fed from the society of which
> he is a part if he will continue fertile.

The rock Williams has chosen for his woman is indeed a most
appropriate symbol by which to express metamorphosis, since the
geological sense of that term is the one which comes first to many
minds; in geology, metamorphosis means a change of forms without
essential change of the ingredients of a rock. Thus it is fully as
important a symbol as water, and united to it in that water is the
chief agent of metamorphosis; *metamorphism* and *metamorphosis*
are used interchangeably. Taken from a large-scale view, the very
world we live in is a natural result of metamorphosis; when that
view is reduced, the circulation of water on, in, and above our
earth becomes merely a figure of the human blood stream, the
blood of Paterson. Again, water as the scientist regards it is the
active principle as against the passive rock that endures the changes
which water brings about.

As the book proceeds, Paterson's thoughts are again the city-

[12] *Briarcliff Quarterly*, III (October 1946), 208.

dwellers: the two lovers who sit talking, a mental defective who writes a letter signed T., a mysterious person afraid of being murdered, a shopper for groceries who shows off a new set of teeth. Williams comes back to the tenet that his thought, though multiple, is also one, "his whole concept"—composed of "the divisions and imbalances" of the facts that constitute Paterson as city. By adding up particulars, he hopes to arrive at the general, an idea expressed figuratively by the Society for Useful Manufactures (S. U. M.) whose factories cluster below the Passaic Falls. All opposites (and the Preface alone contains many: beginning, end; drunk, sober; illustrious, gross; ignorance, knowledge; up, down; addition, subtraction; Pater, son) are reducible somehow to one—"by multiplication a reduction to one." This idea is not new in Williams: in 1934 he addresses scientists thus:

> And you poor fishes haven't yet understood that one plus one plus one plus one plus one equals not five but one. A thing every artist has known from the beginning of time, so thoroughly inescapable that even science is beginning at last to catch on to it.[13]

The second section of Book One closes with a letter from a literary man who signs himself E. D., warning Paterson the poet about the impossibility of dividing book and man. It is just this separation which the poet has been trying to bridge, in his effort to show the interpenetration of the two Patersons, the external with the internal:

> Yet there is
> no return: rolling up out of chaos,
> a nine months' wonder, the city
> the man, an identity—it can't be
> otherwise—an
> interpenetration, both ways.

Another correspondent, a woman initialed C., also accuses him of dividing art and life, of keeping them strictly apart. One feels sympathy with the recipient of the two letters, together with an awareness that he cannot be completely exonerated from the charge, as his own frequent admissions of ineffectuality show.

The third part of Book One begins with a picture of Paterson the man, standing in a room outside which snow melts at a regular rate and dreaming of imagined delights. His thoughts become trees, the leaves of which stream rain, a metaphor Williams is to return to later. Throughout seven stanzas the tree figure is elaborated, ending in the simple statement, "Everybody has roots," reminiscent

[13] "Reply to a Young Scientist," *Directions,* I (Autumn 1934), 28.

of Pound's praise of William Carlos Williams as "rooted." Since there are no ideas but in things, Paterson thinks of mouths eating, kissing, spitting, sucking, speaking; of eyes; of silk-producing machines; of pathetic souvenirs such as a comb and nail file in an imitation leather case, or a photograph holder. He fluctuates between the city–man and the city, the man: "Such is the mystery of his one two, one two."

Continuing his metamorphosis, he becomes one of the crowd; getting into his car as he drives with the rest out past the rhubarb farm in the suburbs, to the convent of the Little Sisters of Saint Ann, which he pictures minutely. Then he "shifts his change," reverie turning into narrative as the 1737 earthquake is described. The first book closes with Thought, personified, climbing up like a snail on the wet rocks of the cavern behind the Falls. Earth is not only our mother, but the father of all speech (Pater*son*), the chatterer (Paterson is often spelled Patterson), a chamber private as a skull to which the world has no access and from which man cannot truly know the world. The torrent (the language) pours down before it, hiding it from sun and sight. In the cavern resides the force that gives reality to all external phenomena:

> And the myth
> that holds up the rock,
> that holds up the water thrives there—
> in that cavern, that profound cleft,
> a flickering green
> inspiring terror, watching . .

Time, in the traditional symbol of the serpent, is the fact that makes real the physical universe.

One sees quite clearly, at this stage of the poem, what metaphysical premises Williams prefers, an idealism which involves a curious ambivalence of beliefs for one to whom the importance of red wheelbarrows, plums, and white chickens (representative sensory detail) looms so large. As far back as the early years of *Poetry,* he was propounding a similar doctrine: "The world of the senses lies unintelligible on all sides. It is only interpretable by the emotions. It only exists when its emotion is fastened to it." [14] The emotion with which the first book closes is one of terror—terror at the sight of the father of all speech (Paterson) standing shrouded amid the din of the Falls, locked away from the secret of salvation. In the Word alone is life, and the contemporary Paterson feels that Word to be inaccessible.

[14] "Notes from a Talk on Poetry," *Poetry,* XIV (July 1919), 213.

For a Redeeming Language

by Denis Donoghue

To teach: to delight: to move. Cicero's three 'offices' of the ora-
tor: a formula ample enough to sustain most literary discussions,
especially the basic ones, as when we would enquire what a writer,
now in his seventies, has been up to all along. The writer, on the
present occasion, is William Carlos Williams: by profession an
obstetrician; by vocation and devotion, a poet who has spent his
life trying to bring new things into the world, to give new names
—exact names—to things that have been long obscured under
old misappellations. Teaching, delighting, moving: sometimes one
of these, occasionally and richly all three together.

To teach: a basic duty, to have something to say. Williams has
had plenty to say, mostly about language, and things, and women,
and formal invention, and divorce, and the American rôle in cul-
ture, and 'the poem as a field of action'. Much of what he has had
to say has been against the grain: hence his sentences, more often
than not, are strokes of an axe: hence also his refusal to lay down
the axe, even when urged to do so by friendship, diplomacy,
orthodoxy, urbanity, or the inertia of English readers. Williams
has been swinging that axe for many years now; which means,
inevitably, that he has written too much, heaping up a profusion
of material now urgently in need of sifting. One of these days an
enterprising publisher will bring out a *Selected Writings:* it should
contain (from the poems) 'The Widow's Lament in Springtime';
'The Hunter'; 'To Waken An Old Lady'; 'Raleigh was Right';
'Burning the Christmas Greens'; *Paterson* (all of it, though there
is a weakening of muscle in the later books); 'To Daphne and
Virginia'; 'TheYachts'; 'These'; and 'Two Pendants'. Also *In the
American Grain* (every word of it), plus 'The Writers of the
American Revolution', the two essays on Marianne Moore, 'The
American Background', and the remarkable review of *A Draft of*

"For a Redeeming Language." From *The Twentieth Century*, CLXIII (June
1958), 532-42. Reprinted by permission of *The Twentieth Century*.

XXX Cantos. It should include a few of the short stories, notably 'Comedy Entombed', some pieces from *Kora in Hell* (to exhibit one of his extremes) and, from the *Letters,* those to Kay Boyle (1932), his son Bill (*circa* September 1942), Horace Gregory (May 1944), Norman Macleod (July 1945), Sister Bernetta Quinn (August 1951), Richard Eberhart (May 1954) and Ezra Pound (November 1956). There is a splendid book in that.

One of the deepest urgencies in Williams is his piety toward *things,* the plenitude of things, their value in being as they are. Hence his delight in finding, in the poems of Marianne Moore, that an apple remains an apple whether it be in Eden or a fruit-bowl; that it is not called upon to yield up its solid, tactile being so that it can take on the smears of mystery. Miss Moore is a guarantor of being, gently refusing to will the actual out of existence for the sake of a poetical transcendence which she would probably find—in any case—a mess. Williams admires her for that. For the same reason he prefers, in Wallace Stevens, the early, opulent poems, probably because the opulence was not *fat* but a glowing testament to the richness of things. For his own pious attachment to the actual, Williams has needed a certain kind of language, a language near to things, closing the gap between subject and object, cutting away all the distorting *nebula* from feelings and attitudes. Above all, a language that will redeem us (he hopes) from past fixations: 'No creed but clarity'. Williams would be pleased to feel that he, like Miss Moore, has spent years wiping soiled words or cutting them clean out, removing the aureoles that have been pasted about them, or taking them bodily from greasy contexts. He has no interest in Beauty.

Only in Language, in Speech, and in what greasy speech does to our lives. Williams has taken as a paradigm of this tragedy the fall of Sam Patch, the great diver whose body, in the supreme test, wavered when he jumped 125 feet from the falls of the Genesee River on November 13, 1826. His body wavered in the air: speech had failed him: 'the word had been drained of its meaning'. Which we would translate to include the defeat of communication, the divorce of art from life, the boiling of pearls, the corruption of society. Sam Patch failed; we succumb to a degraded sense of the Word. In 'Convivio' Williams refers to

> the liars who decree laws
> with no purpose other than to make a screen
> of them for larceny, murder—for our

> murder, we who salute the word and would
> have it clean, full of sharp movement.

Williams has always recognized his enemies, and it is part of his
rhetoric to insist that they must be ours too if we are to redeem
ourselves. Knowing this we share his motive:

> I must
> find my meaning and lay it, white,
> beside the sliding water: myself—
> comb out the language—or succumb.

This language which Williams seeks, at its simplest it is a lan-
guage agile in providing vivid simulations of the thing seen, done,
said, suffered. But in its severest test it must yield up the new
thing made, not the managed poem but the Invention. And there
is nothing iconoclastic about this. Williams knows that poems
quite unlike his own have been written and that some of them
are masterpieces; he knows that and glories in it. What he wants
is A NEW MEASURE CONSONANT WITH OUR DAY. He has spoken of 'an
approach to a possible continent, such poems as would signalize
a complete break with the past, fit to lay beside the work of the
past which they would thus affirm by their newness'. And again:
'It may be said that I wish to destroy the past. It is precisely a
service to tradition, honoring it and serving it that is envisioned
and intended by my attack, and not disfigurement—confirming and
enlarging its application'. What he wants is that invention which
will clarify our time and, in its integrity, enact a tribute to other
inventions in other times:

> Let the snake wait under
> his weed
> and the writing
> be of words, slow and quick, sharp
> to strike, quiet to wait,
> sleepless.
>
> —through metaphor to reconcile
> the people and the stones.
> Compose. (No ideas
> but in things) Invent!
> Saxifrage is my flower that splits
> the rocks.

True, Williams has sometimes imagined he saw saxifrage when he was looking at, say, the poems of Rexroth, and he probably sees in Eli Siegel one of the Chosen Few. But we need not hold him too closely to account for these mirages; they do not disprove the value of a flower that splits rocks.

Nor do they provide an excuse for ignoring Williams. A man who sets out to write the moral history of his country may be allowed a few local errors. Besides, what is crucial is the motive of the endeavour, and its direction. It is absurd to think that Williams has been wasting fifty years in a one-sided battle with Europe; there is no shadow-boxing here. What he has been fighting is not Europe herself but America's reluctance to see her own true image. He fights not to destroy Europe but to define America. Hence he emphasizes one pattern of early American experience out of many, the conflict between 'reliance on the prevalent conditions of place and the overriding of an unrelated authority', Europe. The American effort, he argues, has been to appraise the real through the maze of a cut-off and imposed culture from Europe. (I imagine if Williams were to endorse any particular slant in American historical scholarship it would be Frederick Jackson Turner's, in *The Significance of the Frontier in American History*.) Hence his exaltation of those writers who, like himself, have declared their American Independence; notably Freneau, Poe, Whitman:

> In America we had and still have an unformed, more or less anonymous language which, among our writers, Whitman was the first to perceive and to act upon with firmness and decision—to break down the old forms . . .

Thus Williams at a very late stage in a tradition of self-conscious nationality that goes back beyond Samuel Adams; it includes Bryant, Channing, Emerson, Poe, Whitman, Melville, and several writers up to Mencken. Here is Melville in the essay on Hawthorne:

> Let us away with this leaven of literary flunkeyism toward England. If either must play the flunkey in this thing, let England do it, not us.

The teaching had become belligerent at that stage: Williams is more careful with the facts. No chauvinist:

> Because a thing is American or related to the immediate conditions it is not therefore to be preferred to the finished product of another culture.

What he wants is the finished product of American culture; and there is no denying his own contribution to that end. To read widely in his work is to realize that he has done something new in American literature; something which he (though not the greatest poet in the language) was able to do because he saw what had to be done and the time was ripe: he had the luck, and just enough talent to seize the chance. Hugh Kenner has described it, with American vigour:

> Dr Williams is the first American writer to discover, not the phases of America that reflect what was in Europe, but the core of America that is itself, new, and so far unvocal.

The core, the source, the root: this is the concern of *In the American Grain,* many of the *Essays,* of *Paterson,* and *The Great American Novel.* The people of *Paterson* move around, without motive, inarticulate, because they do not understand themselves, not understanding their origin, their source. Williams is concerned to show that there is something under the soil, roots which (understood) give new life and meaning. Hence his unacademic resuscitations of Columbus, Cortez, the founding of Quebec, the *Mayflower,* Aaron Burr; his inspired cribbing from Cotton Mather, from Franklin's *Information to those who would remove to America,* from William Nelson's *History of the City of Paterson and the County of Passaic.* Hence his devoted elucidation of James Otis, Patrick Henry, William Bartram, Crèvecoeur, Freneau, his hymns to Jefferson, Franklin, Washington and (in his own world) Alfred Stieglitz. But history does not explain everything; there is still, as part of the core, the irrational, the things we have to include to represent all we do not understand. So, in *Paterson,* Williams inserts a few letters which have nothing to do with the 'story', but which are qualitatively apt, standing for the impalpable *something* which inhabits the real. It all fits in.

But where? And how? Many readers of Williams have felt that he is too short on organization, on large-scale manipulations issuing from a coherent penetration of experience. True, his manipulations often seem to be fragmentary epiphanies (as in 'The Red Wheelbarrow') and yet I should be surprised to find that they are not determined by some Idea, some Universal, of which they are partial enactments. Recall that it was Williams who wrote:

> It is hard to say what makes a poem good, but if it is not in the detail of its construction, it is in nothing. If the detail of the construction is not to the smallest particular distinguished, the whole poem might as well be thrown out.

It is difficult to reconcile this with the great big lumpkin who, we are told, wouldn't be caught dead in the company of an idea. There is on my side the evidence of such poems as 'Tract', 'These', 'Dedication for a Plot of Ground', 'The Lonely Street', 'A Coronal'. There is Williams' life-long devotion to craft, to measure, to the resources of speech, to a redeeming language. And behind all this there is his vigorous idea of culture. Just listen to him talking about it:

> The burning need of a culture is not a choice to be made or not made, voluntarily, any more than it can be satisfied by loans. It has to be where it arises, or everything related to the life there ceases. It isn't a thing: it's an act. If it stands still, it is dead. It is the realization of the qualities of a place in relation to the life which occupies it; embracing everything involved, climate, geographic position, relative size, history, other cultures—as well as the character of its sands, flowers, minerals and the condition of knowledge within its borders. It is the act of lifting these things into an ordered and utilized whole which is culture. It isn't something left over afterward. That is the record only. The act is the thing.

This is not the writing of a fuddy-duddy; these are deep matters, to be ignored at our peril, and Williams refuses to ignore them. In fact, what he has undertaken to provide (in poems, essays, fiction, drama) is a grammar of American culture; American because that is what he has at hand and knows best and cares most about, not because he thinks it the richest culture ever achieved. I do not claim that it is a perfect grammar; it omits too much, despite its profusion. For one thing, to place beside it Eliot's *Notes towards the Definition of Culture* is to see that Williams' grammar lacks a focal religious perspective; and I am of Eliot's party in this respect. But I revere Williams—and Stevens—for what they have carved out from what they had in hand; without evasion or falsification. A Grammar of Culture without benefit of Clergy: I have no temptation to sneer.

*　　*　　*

To delight: 'style is ingratiation'. Williams' best poems delight the mind because they penetrate the behaviour of things by means of a language lithe, actual, close to the behaviour of speech. Chaucer, Wyatt, Greville, Browning, Pound; but Williams needed the support of someone nearer home, Whitman, someone who would sustain him in the belief that the diction and idiom and pronunciation of American speech constituted a new language, American as distinct from English and sometimes as opposed to

English. And Williams would say, as Whitman said in a passage which Mencken cited as a slogan in *The American Language:*

> The appetite of the people of These States, in popular speeches and writings, is for unhemmed latitude, coarseness, directness, live epithets, expletives, words of opprobrium, resistance . . . I like limber, lasting, fierce words.

Williams has picked up these words nearby:

> I live where I live and acknowledge no lack of opportunity because of that to be alert to facts, to the music of events, of words, of the speech of people about me. As well as to the speech of the muse, the intangible perfection of all excellent verse.

The task in hand, then—to use this speech as substance of a new measure consonant with our day, not for the 'music' but for the sake of modes of consciousness otherwise dumb: 'It is in the newness of a live speech that the new line exists undiscovered'.

That was twenty-five years ago. Williams now believes that he has discovered this new measure, that he happened on it in *Paterson II,* the passage beginning

> The descent beckons
> > as the ascent beckoned
> > > Memory is a kind
>
> of accomplishment

What does it amount to? Here is a recent passage, from 'To Daphne and Virginia':

> The smell of the heat is boxwood
> > when rousing us
> > > a movement of the air
> stirs our thoughts
> > that had no life in them
> > > to a life, a life in which
> two women agonize:
> > to live and to breathe is no less.
> > > Two young women.
> The box odor
> > Is the odor of that of which
> > > partaking separately,
> each to herself
> > I partake also
> > > . . separately.

Williams counts each of these short lines as a foot. What he wants
is 'a *relatively* stable foot, not a rigid one', a foot expanded to
allow a freer handling of the measure. He talks a lot about Einstein,
and there I do not understand him, though I assume he knows
his man. To my ear the only thing the lines of the new measure
have in common is duration, and the determining factor would
seem to be that the measure moves in phrases, close to speech,
with the free movement of the rhetorical stresses as counterpoint.
Or so I understand it. The words have the movement, the pattern,
of bars in music; each bar may contain any number of syllables,
in keeping with the tendency of the language (even the English
language!) 'to squeeze units into relatively equal time spans'. The
pattern gets its dynamics, after this, from the discreet use of
internal rhymes, assonance, complex alliteration, and pauses. Thus
the pause of depressed insight before the second 'separately'; the
defining of the life of Daphne and Virginia as a weathering of
agones. Again:

> I have two sons,
>   the husbands of these women,
>   who live also
> in a world of love,
>   apart.
>   Shall this odor of box in
>   the heat
>   not also touch them
>   fronting a world of women
>   from which they are
>   debarred
>   by the very scents which draw them on
>   against easy access?

This is verse at least as well written as distinguished prose. The
measure is just sufficiently *there* to enforce discipline and to en-
sure that the writing (and the consciousness behind it) will be
scrupulous, exact. And the pattern, established, allows Williams
to lay down the single, final word 'apart' and to have its bar
filled up with a pause of sorrowful recognition, without rancour.
And there is the quite different load placed upon 'debarred'. Wil-
liams is using a measure not to intensify but to control, to test the
feeling as it meets the edge of the language. In Kenner's version:
'That the cadence in which words move controls the degree of
meaning they yield up, and that words set in Jersey speech rhythms

mean less but mean it with greater finality, is Williams' chief technical perception'.

The 'propriety of cadence' which Charles Tomlinson has admired in Williams is a constant delight. And I am gratified too by Williams' touching faith—even though I do not share it—that everything he sees, hears, tastes, is important for that very reason. Everything *is* important, but not because of a chance encounter with Williams' senses. And yet a poet had better have that excess than any other, even if it spawns a few pretentious trivia like 'The Young Housewife'. Williams' life-work is, among other things, a huge diary which like most diaries contains a certain proportion of expendable matter; the thing to do with these notations (such as 'The Locust Tree in Flower', or 'This Is Just To Say') is to read them with sympathy and pass on. Likewise when, as in 'Ballad of Faith', Williams is spitting out his latest obsessions just to be rid of the taste.

The man is only human, and his humanity is a delight. Also his willingness to risk moving from strongholds. Williams probably remained an Imagist longer than his reputation could well afford, and there are some readers who still feel that they need only affix the label and move off. True, many of his poems proceed under their own impetus (and its pride) as a phalanx of concretions, and lest there should be any unpleasantness between Image and Idea, Williams generally lets it be known that Image is his favourite son and that, if necessary, he will intervene on his behalf. He is a very Kantian poet indeed. But in the best poems there is no disagreement between the two; in 'To Waken An Old Lady', or 'These', or 'The Widow's Lament in Springtime'. In such poems the concretions are there in all their richness, and the Idea is accorded plenary enactment.

Much of Williams' writing is sharp, assertive; he rarely tries to persuade by appearing urbane; if he has a bedside manner he keeps it for his patients. But even in his prose—which he writes to discourage our persistence in error—he often writes with remarkable tenderness. Here is part of the prose elegy called 'The American Background':

> It was Jefferson who, when President, would walk to his office in the mud, out of principle, and walk home again ignoring the mud, as against the others who would ride. And at the same time it was Jefferson who, recognizing the imperious necessity for other loveliness to lay beside his own, such as it was, would inquire whether or not it might be possible, in securing a gardener, to get one who could at

the same time play the flute. His home at Monticello, with its original-
ity, good taste, with its distinctive local quality, is one of the few
places where the two cultural strains approach in our history, where
they consciously draw together. But Jefferson's idea would be sadly
snowed under.

*   *   *

To teach, to delight, to move: I have a little theory about
Williams which may explain—if nothing else—why I find his work
moving. He seems to me, despite all contrary indications, a
Paleface, very much a highbrow (witness his committed devotion
to the craft of language, the nearest modern equivalent of Henry
James on fiction)—but a Paleface dissatisfied with this condition
because it seems somehow a bit thin, a bit too English, too far
removed from a local, immediate American context. Hence his
rush to exalt the Redskin, the frontiersman, taking this warmer
role unto himself by *fiat.* Hence his reluctance to effect a direct
entry to ideas—except in necessary polemic. Hence his distrust
of urbanity, his distaste for 'Rev. Eliot', his snarling essays (sound-
ing off), his insistence on making discussions of literature earthy,
barbaric, sexy. It is my understanding that Williams, by tempera-
ment, is closer to Henry James than to Whitman, and that his
dissatisfaction with this temper makes him adopt the accoutre-
ments of Daniel Boone. Daniel Boone was a fine man too.

It is a moving predicament. What Williams admires is, deep
down, what we all admire—achievement. Williams *moves* his
audience not by hoisting himself to a Grand Style but by offering
instances, mainly from American history, of exceptional achieve-
ment. What he seeks, what we seek, is an image of *wholeness,* of
'perfection', and even an image of heroic failure will serve. *In
the American Grain* has Franklin, Columbus, Boone, Washington,
Lincoln. *Paterson IV* has Madame Curie to take the place of Yeats's
Major Gregory. 'Two Pendants' has 'Elena'. And, outside the
poems, there is Herbert Clark, a princely example, devoting his
life to the elimination of the yellow fever mosquito in the Central
American jungle. And there are others.

Williams' writing, then, has body, substance; he has no interest
in finding different ways of saying precious little. There are large
issues involved which he understands better than most. Part of
what he understands, part of what he teaches, is that life is im-
portant, that human beings are important, that the dignity of
a human being depends on his power of moral choice. I cannot
cite chapter and verse for this, but it seems to me to be deeply

involved in his work. It sounds traditional, and perhaps Williams is more traditional than we have assumed. True, by temperament he is more interested in achieving the new than in making obeisance to the old, but he knows the difference between being emancipated and being merely unbuttoned. He wants freedom but not Caliban's freedom; he wants freedom to invent new forms, epiphanies of our time. And surely there can be few things more moving than the labour of such a man toward clarity, self-knowledge, understanding.

"A Certainty of Music": Williams' Changes

by Richard A. Macksey

Like Père Sebastian Rasles in the wilderness, William Carlos Williams starts out overland to touch and to baptize. Williams early dispossesses himself of his romantic inheritance, its epistemological obsessions as well as its seminal metaphors of alienation. He sees no need for escape or for evasion; any transcendence beyond the immediate field of experience is unthinkable. There are no magic casements opening on another world nor elfin grots that lead to heaven's bourne. "The dumfoundering abyss/Between us and the object" no longer exists for Williams. What he retains from the tradition, as Wallace Stevens pointed out, is a certain generosity and spontaneity of the affections, a readiness of sentiment, held in check by the clarity of observation and precision of expression. Stevens sees his friend as a happier Laocoön, completely engaged with immediate experience yet struggling to retain his identity through the artful construction of the poem. This ready capability of entering intimately into an object or scene is reminiscent of Keats, his earliest model; but the ecstatic sensory encounter for the romantic poet is always achieved at the expense of self, which dissolves into an empathic union with things. To this passionate renunciation of the individual, Williams opposes a positively willful voice, naming and touching and tasting his new world. The compassionate but assured physician probes and palps the body of his patient.

For Williams, as for Whitman, the encounter with the world is one of *contact;* the initial experience is local and intimate. The old quandaries about the nature of the self vanish in the energetic act of apprehending and verifying the rampant local world which surrounds the poet. He defines himself in the very act of celebrat-

---

"'A Certainty of Music': Williams' Changes" has not been published before. It is part of a longer essay on the full evolution of Williams' work.

ing the diversity and plenitude of this immediate world.[1] The covenant with nature is sealed by the poet's active possession of reality's diverse inventory. Everywhere his alert senses meet with a certain resistance and with an amazing denseness. Objects, gestures, and even speech—wiped clean of the "greasy stains" of habit—seem to have a palpable kinesthetic firmness. In this "savage and tender" intimacy, even light, "that rocks to and fro" and "drips from leaf to leaf," [2] has an objective body like some congealing fluid. From the constant pressure of the inquiring poet and this local resistance spring tensions and the awareness of incessant movement, arrested only by the muscular exertion of the poem itself. The poem, which in its presentation and composition of the flux of particulars is a model of the initial possession, alone promises a momentary stay against the ceaseless cycle of change.

The poem, too, is a local place, "a field of force," which the imagination of the poet inhabits and composes. The imagination is heuristic, discovering in every fresh encounter with the commonplace a new frontier of human significance. Williams' poet, like F. J. Turner's American pioneer, must master this frontier.

---

[1] Williams' resurgent optimism, which conquers his doubts about urban America, could be related to this principle of plenitude in a universe of continuous becoming. A. O. Lovejoy has explored the consequences of a delight in plenitude for a world where "the great chain" has been temporalized into a process of increasing diversification. Even conflict could be absorbed into the design: "The traditional argument for optimism in all ages . . . represented the Cosmic Artist as cramming his canvas with diversified detail to the last infinitesimal fraction of a inch; as caring far more for the fullness and variety of content than for simplicity and perfection of form; and as seeking this richness of coloring and abundance of contrast even at the cost of disharmony, irregularity, and what appears to us as confusion." *The Great Chain of Being* (Cambridge: Harvard University Press, 1936), pp. 296-97. For Williams, it is the human artist's task to *impose* the "perfection of form" on this emerging plenitude.

[2] The following texts of Williams' work have been used in this essay. Each is accompanied by the abbreviation which will be used in citations. KH—*Kora in Hell: Improvisations* (San Francisco: City Lights Books, 1957); SA—*Spring and All* (Dijon: Contact Publishing Company, 1923); IAG—*In the American Grain* (New York: Albert & Charles Boni, 1925); CEP—*The Collected Earlier Poems* (New York: New Directions Publishing Corporation, 1951); A—*The Autobiography of William Carlos Williams* (New York: Random House, 1951); SE—*Selected Essays* (New York: Random House, 1954); SL—*Selected Letters*, ed. John C. Thirlwall (New York: Ivan Obolensky, Inc., 1957); IWWP—*I Wanted to Write a Poem: The Autobiography of the Works of a Poet*, recorded and edited by Edith Heal (Boston: Beacon Press, 1958); CLP—*The Collected Later Poems*, revised edition (New York: New Directions Publishing Corporation, 1963); P—*Paterson* (New York: New Directions Publishing Corporation, 1963). The initial quotations are from CEP, 194 and 173.

He makes a start out of particulars "so that in looking at some apparently small object one feels the swirl of great events" (SE, 294). The agency of this imaginative mastery lies precisely in words, themselves ordered in space as the measured stresses and junctures of speech compose a figured dance. Forming new figures in print, these words are held in tension on the page as in a new field of force. The words are in a certain sense "abstracted" from the objects they describe, just as the measure is a pattern more or less abstracted from the rhythms of natural speech. Together words and rhythmic patterns are disposed in a new space where the poet "constructs" a new object, the poem. This new object is governed by rigid economies of image, syntax, line, and measure which compress the rout of experience into an instant fixity. Unlike the cosmic expansions of Whitman's strophe it retains its objective firmness and guarantees "the animate touch" between the poet and his reader, sacrificing the identity of neither. One title suggests the compressive energy of the poetic activity: "The World Contracted to a Recognizable Image." Williams early described the independent existence of the poem as a solid nexus between poet, world, and reader in one of the prose passages of *Spring and All:*

> Imagination is not to avoid reality, nor is it description nor an evocation of objects or situations, it is to say that poetry does not tamper with the world but moves it—It affirms reality most powerfully and therefore, since reality needs no personal support but exists free from human action . . . it creates a new object, a play, a dance which is not a mirror up to nature but—   (SA, 91)

It was Williams' life work to complete the sentence by example,

> . . . to dance to a measure
> contrapuntally,
>   Satyrically, the tragic foot.   (P, 278)

The world of discrete particulars which the poet's eye "seizes," which his other hungry senses grasp and savor, and which he certifies with his totemic poem, is immediate in time as well as place: it is the familiar landscape of everyday and it is constantly coming into being and passing away, often with a violence that astonishes the beholder. In the rôle of natural and human physician, Williams attends these self-renewing births and deaths, as alert to "the stark dignity of/entrance," which quickens spring, as to the final agonies of the rubbish heap aflame in the dead weeds, which marks the descent of winter. Amidst this constant change he goes his rounds, delivering the nascent phrase or gesture in its unsoiled originality or probing the "drab trash" of a dying culture, the compost of his scarred urban scenes. Things are never lost, only transformed. The ground itself is time compressed and compacted to inert stone where geological layers of the past can be exposed by the rock drill, the persistent saxifrage, or the poem. All time is thus flattened out and stratified, but it is the ground from which Williams' recurrent symbols of life, the humble flowers of North Jersey, "slender green/reaching up from sand and rubble," push their way as they grip the soil (CLP, 28). The poet's imagination, too, is a flower, at once violent and gentle, which can grip and push and "milk stones" (CLP, 195); the present moment, however unpromising, is the surface soil from which it must flower.

Anywhere will do, so long as it is immediately present to the embracing senses; and any time will do, so long as it is now. Poet and poem are rooted in the ubiquitous soil of the present; together they share the perilous brevity of the flower. Each poetic act raises an articulate structure against the sprawling chaos of universal flux. There is no temporal depth to the experience or to the poem. Time past can only be represented spatially, as a collage of juxtaposed presents. In this temporal as well as spatial contraction into an indestructible moment, as well as in the extraordinary tactility of consciousness, Williams' poetry resembles that of a contemporary poet whom he admired and translated, René Char. Both are rooted in the particularities of their environment and moment; both see a vital transfer of energy in the willful compression of time and place into the poetic "object"; both increasingly embody their aesthetics in love poems of intense directness.[3] Although both could be said to use a "poésie crispée" as the stay against the volatility of experience, Williams, however, lacks the radical insecurity of the poet of the Vaucluse. Char can speak of himself as "magicien de l'insécurité . . . centre toujours inachevée," rescuing his enterprise only briefly by a supreme act of the will from cosmic disaster; while the remarkable assurance of Williams, his ability to accept the shocks of the immediate with a minimum of alarm was early recognized by his friend Marianne Moore. He moves easily in his world of abrupt and violent change, adjusting his reponse to the moment.

[3] See Georges Poulet, *Le Point de départ: Études sur le temps humain: III* (Paris: Plon, 1964), pp. 92-99. It is interesting to compare Williams' expression of his poetics in Paterson III, Section 3 ("The Burning of the Library") with Char's *La Bibliothèque est en feu* (Paris: Louis Broder, 1956).

Often human time seems for Williams to describe the same
self-renewing reversals which primitive man associated with the
polar oppositions in nature; day–night, summer–winter, birth–
death: not as duration but as metamorphosis. Just as man invades
and subjugates his environment, fragments of past experience
invade the poet's present as alien visitors and are welcomed:

> The very old past was refound
> redirected. It had wandered into himself
> The world was himself. . . .   (CEP, 306)

Secure in his command of the poetic field, Williams can order and
juxtapose these scraps of time with the same authority that he
exercises over objects. (And so he is able to extend his momentary
poetry beyond the dimensions of Char's "poèmes pulvérisés.")
Williams may have learned this montage of times and places on
a continuous pictorial plane from the experiments of Gris and
the other Cubist painters whom he early championed. As in the
"static action" of their painting, everything must be present
within the field at once and the poem cannot depend upon any
doctrine of correspondence or technique of indirection; the "reso-
nances" must be all present to the view. As early as the Prologue
to *Kora in Hell* Williams argued that "the coining of similes is
a pastime of very low order, depending as it does upon a nearly
vegetable coincidence. Much more keen is that power which dis-
covers in things those inimitable particles of dissimilarity to all
other things which are the peculiar perfections of the thing in
question" (SE, 16). The operative word here is the active verb
"discovers," which suggests both the variety and the vigor of
Williams' enterprise.

The "peculiar perfections" which the poet discovers are born
out of strenuous oppositions (although never the romantic op-
position of subject and object). The mind of the poet, that "queer
sponge" of which he speaks in "May 1st Tomorrow," assimilates
them all and utters them forth again under the vigorous squeezing
which is the creative process. The perfection of the flower declares
itself against the formless rubble from which it grows: "Milkweed,
a single stalk on the bare/embankment" (CLP, 28). The male
poet or sparrow assertively defines himself as he waltzes before
his determined mate. The polarities are founded in a cosmology
of elemental opposition between the formless "ground" of anarchic
muck and the achieved form of flowers and gestures and poems.
Objects are for Williams "nodes of energy" in a field of force.
Between the two poles flows the transforming energy, both creative

and destructive, of the "radiant gist." It is this daemonic force, an animism in nature and the imagination in the poet, which can convert matter into energy and a desolate field into the vibrant "white desire" of Queen-Anne's-Lace. As his insistent floral imagery suggests, for Williams the oppositions can be understood in sexual terms, with the animistic principle, the radioactive "fire," flowing between male and female, between form and matrix, between creation and destruction. The fire is the transforming imagination of the poet entering and commanding, but it is also the flame which releases a new beauty in "Burning the Christmas Greens" and in *Paterson III*, Section 3.

Many readers have noticed the peculiar facility with which Williams assumes feminine as well as masculine roles in his poetry and fiction. This androgynous character of his imagination is a clue to the assurance with which he moves from the fury of the "big she-Wop" and her "catastrophic birth" to the stillness of "the male mind, nesting," curiously imitating maternal instincts in the creative process (CLP, 8, 195). The completeness with which Williams can inhabit the most intimate feminine experience, his ability to move freely from images of formative masculine desire to the volcanic matrix of motherhood, can perhaps be traced genetically to the profound influences of his mediating profession and the extraordinary women who animate his life—his grandmother, his mother, and his wife. But structurally these movements can be understood as an expression of his triadic cosmology. He seems to locate the personality, as it finds life in the imagination, as flowing ceaselessly between the ground and the form which struggles from it. This mobile and vital force with which he identifies his existence is reminiscent of the Greek model for the deathless soul.[4] While the quintessential soul or psyche exists in the living as semen or marrow, it survives the body in the chthonic form of the snake worshipped by the ancestor cults. It is this snake, or congealed semen, which can pass from life to death or, in coitus, from man to woman. The process is one of continuous deaths and births between polar oppositions. As the Cambridge anthropologists have suggested, the cosmic oppositions of feminine earth (Gaea) and masculine sky (Ouranos), the primal gods of life, can be seen in terms of this seminal image of passage: the rain which falls and rises is the cosmic semen which engenders all

[4] See R. B. Onians, *Origins of European Thought* (Cambridge, England: Cambridge University Press, 1951) and Jane Harrison, *Prolegomena to the Study of Greek Religion* (3rd ed.; Cambridge, England: Cambridge University Press, 1922).

things. In "Raindrops on a Briar" Williams figures the tense juncture of "the thinking male" and the "charged and deliver/ing female" in this same mediating symbol, "a more pregnant motion" (CLP, 99). The Greek notion of "cosmic ages" seems to stem from this oscillation of force between opposites. While rain is the semen of Zeus, the transforming fire is the semen of Hephaestos the artisan. And the offerings of safe passage for the dead were *panspermia,* baskets of seeds and phallic emblems.[5] The figure of Greek mythology who most clearly represents the role of Williams as poet is the enigmatic Hermes, guardian of the dead in their journeys to and from the underworld, inventor of the lyre, and irrepressible trickster. His very name seems to be derived from the heap of stones (ἕρμα) which marked the magic boundaries between two realms; his earliest representations were ithyphallic stones.[6] Norman O. Brown has summarized what we know of his psychography and has attempted to show the intimate relation in all the metamorphoses of Hermes between the phallus which was his body, and later his staff, and his transforming functions as magician, craftsman, and god of boundaries and trade.[7]

Like Hermes, the poet is in perpetual transit between the polarities of his world. He is the "radioactive gist" which, in a post-Einsteinian world, stands for the constant seminal exchanges of Greek cosmology. And, in Edmund R. Leach's brilliant gloss on Aristotle's *de Mundo,* Chapter 7, where Kronos stands as a representation of Chronos (Eternal Time), we have a model for Williams' own experience of endless temporality.[8] The role of

[5] Jane Harrison, *Themis* (Cambridge, England: Cambridge University Press, 1912).

[6] See L. Preller, *Griechische Mythologie,* 4th ed., rev. C. Robert (Berlin: Weidmann, 1894-1926), I, 401; also L. R. Farnell, *Cults of the Greek States* (Oxford: The Clarendon Press, 1896-1909), V, 7; N. M. P. Nilsson, *Griechische Feste* (Leipzig: B. G. Teubner, 1906), 388; Ibid., *A History of Greek Religion,* trans. F. J. Fielden (Oxford: The Clarendon Press, 1925), pp. 109-10; U. von Wilamowitz-Moellendorff, *Der Glaube der Hellenen* (Berlin: Weidmannsche Buchhandlung, 1931-32), I, 159.

[7] Hermes was the "god of doors," the "guide" and "ambassador" who protects men in all traffic with strangers. On Hermes as god of communication see Farnell, *Cults,* V, 66-67; N. O. Brown, *Hermes the Thief* (Madison: University of Wisconsin Press, 1947), Chapter 2.

[8] Edmund R. Leach, *Rethinking Anthropology* (London: University of London, Athlone Press, 1961), pp. 124-32. In his penetrating essay Mr. Leach connects the myth of Kronos (the beginning of life and the end of life out of cosmic opposition) with the structural paradigms of Radcliffe-Brown for the identification of alternating generations and of Lévi-Strauss for the algebra of marriage alliances.

Kronos, child of earth and sky in the gory myth, describes for the first time the cosmic oscillation between generations, between procreation and castration, between polar elements of human life. The opposed figures of male and female give birth to a world of becoming where life and death of individual generations succeed each other as with the motion of the shuttle, but where the vital, mobile principle lives in a constant present and possesses each in turn.

II

In a poetry of unmediated and instantaneous sensation, what possibility can be found for development in the range of subject and in the elaboration of experience? The poet does not proceed by any intellectual dialectics and his time would seem to have no depth, only constant oscillation: he and the poem live in the moment inhabited by the mobile Hermetic energy. And yet, over a half century of writing, Williams demonstrates a remarkable talent for technical and substantive development. The archaic image of the soul in transit suggests a clue both to his metamorphic imagination and to his evolution. Although early and late a poetry of "presence," Williams' verse describes a series of critical rites of passage. Each rite carries him, almost unconscious, to a new status and a new vantage. Among the successful transitions there is a remarkable similarity of structure which can be analyzed in terms of the classic studies undertaken by Durkheim and his followers of the transition rites of the "moral person." [9] The structure of each transition takes the form of an unqualified plunge into that which the poet is ultimately to apprehend and master, whether it be the independent world of discrete objects, the anarchy of unkenneled speech, or the daemonic self that claps hands and sings behind drawn shades. In each case the rite takes the form of *descent* which means an abandonment and resignation, but in each case it also discloses an access to a new kind of personal utterance and mastery. The plunge is ultimately an *ascent* to an increasing command of the poet's materials. The axiom is one familiar to all obstetricians (although not in the symbolist sense of the formula): the way down is the way up, the violence of

[9] Arnold van Gennep, *Les Rites de passage* (Paris: É. Nourry, 1909), especially chapters 1 and 8; Émile Durkheim, *Les Formes élémentaires de la vie religieuse* (Paris: F. Alcan, 1912); Henri Hubert and Marcel Mauss, "Étude sommaire de la représentation du temps dans la religion et la magie," *Mélanges d'histoire des religions* (Paris: F. Alcan, 1909).

birth releases a new freedom. The trajectory of the passage is charted in *Kora in Hell:*

> Often when the descent seems well marked there will be a subtle ascent over-ruling it so that in the end when the degradation is fully anticipated the person will be found to have emerged upon a hilltop.   (KH, 47)

Each descent appears to be a kind of death, like the descent of Kora-Persephone, the poet's muse; and yet the "dead" seed strains back to life, to "spring and all."

Following the structural analyses of Van Gennep, Hubert, and Mauss, we would expect this fateful plunge to be a rite of *separation,* a movement away from "reality." But the death is always illusory and the experience is more adequately represented by the transitions of birth and marriage. The passage is revealed as a genuine rite of *incorporation* into a still more intimate relation between the poet and the particulars of his world. As we have seen, for Williams there is no "other world" to which he can remove, nor any "sacred time" into which he can withdraw from the profane. Life and death, the "me" and the "not-me" are all co-present in his swarming landscape.

Just as the tragic experience seems to have been grounded in a rite of separation (the hero is increasingly isolated and opaque as he moves toward death), the comic experience suggests rites of incorporation such as marriage, where the hero is reintegrated both into society and into a certain transparency of type. Williams, however tragic he may judge the "divorces" of modern life to be, still reaches for the comic mask and dances on the satyric foot.

Significantly, Williams' career began with a failure to achieve this model rite of incorporation. Even a cursory look at the earliest limbo of imitative "romantic" verse from which Williams emerged suggests the integrity of the subsequent structural transitions. Reading Keats in the Penn Dormitory and during his internship, he labored over a long, uncompleted (and uncompletable) narrative poem. It was a broken series of unachieved passages set in an alien, "literary" world. In his *Autobiography* he describes the vague prince of his narrative as divorced from both time and place, wandering lost in a "romantic past" unable even to understand the language of the place in which he found himself. He was the victim of cancelled rites: his *marriage* had been interrupted and, in the "secondary dream plot," his *death journey* to an alien place resembling Böcklin's "Insel des Todes" was interrupted as well. He was condemned to endless and aimless wandering: "So he went on, homeward or seeking a home that was his own, all this through a 'foreign' country whose language was barbarous" (A, 60).

Nothing could be further removed from the project of a poet who championed the local and immediate. The hero's separation was as total as his author's frustration, which grew while "book followed book," until the frantic young poet finally managed to dispatch the manuscript through the furnace door. Starting from a new beginning, as the *Autobiography* testifies, Williams underwent the first genuine rite of passage immediately thereafter. He turned to a new conception of poetry in the very act of writing the next poem.

This first surviving long poem, "The Wanderer," carries him beyond the alienation implied by the title and records a total immersion. Under the tutelary spirit of his formidable grandmother the hero plunges into the filth of the Passaic River. (Sister Bernetta Quinn had to remind the poet that this was the source which was ultimately to flow into the creation of *Paterson*.) The hero celebrates a ritual marriage from which he emerges refreshed and miraculously possessed of his world. Unlike the earlier Keatsian wanderings, this voyage, in its absolute submission and possession, brings him home.

What flows from this ritual sacrifice of his isolation is the concrete richness of Williams' "imagist" poetry, where the sensuous "contours and the shine/hold the eye" as the "Sea-Trout and Butterfish" dart into sharp definition, separated from the watery matrix:

> The eye comes down eagerly
> unravelled of the sea
>
> separates this from that
> and the fine fins' sharp spines   (CEP, 91)

And yet, in his intensely personal acceptance and affirmation of this world of particulars, Williams has already moved beyond the chastity of the orthodox imagist. His hardness and concentration in the best poems of this period bear the unique mark of his own hand pressing out and touching.

This constant pressure of the poet's identity, responding to the fecund variety of things in the very act of discovering and exploring them, is one clue to the profound assurance as a sensate part of the immediate world which Williams firmly achieved after the nuptial plunge into the filth of the Passaic River. He acknowledges this ritual transition into secure community with other things in an important letter to his friend Marianne Moore:

> The inner security though is an overwhelmingly important observation. . . . It is something which occurred once when I was about twenty, a sudden resignation to existence, a despair—if you wish to call it that, but a despair which made everything a unit and at the same time a part of myself. I suppose it might be called a sort of nameless religious experience. I resigned, I gave up. . . . I won't follow causes. I can't. The reason is that it seems so much more important to me that I *am.* Where shall one go? What shall one do? Things have no names for me and places have no significance. As a reward for this anonymity I feel as much a part of things as trees and stones. Heaven seems frankly impossible. I am damned as I succeed. I have no particular hope save to repair, to rescue, to complete.   (SL, 147)

Williams thus describes his point of departure, without baggage but totally at home in a world which he can both heal and sustain.

Together, *Kora in Hell* (1920) and *Spring and All* (1923) mark a second transformation in Williams' poetic *rites de passage.* The first book marks the phase of descent, figured in the myth of Persephone's exile; while the second celebrates spring's stubborn return as the goddess reclaims the human world. In this passage the poet discovers access to the energies within himself, as they are released to the surface and the touch of things. In *Kora in Hell* Williams abandons the programmatic detachment of the "objective" poet to plunge into the depths of his own unconscious in search of the *duende.* The adventure and certain aspects of the treatment are reminiscent of Rimbaud's nocturnal search for absolute beginnings, and hence reintegration, in *Les Illuminations.* The change in vector represents a considered act of abandonment: the writing will "utter itself." "*While* it is being written, as far as possible, the writer be he mathematician or poet, must with a stored mind no doubt, must nevertheless thoroughly abandon himself to the writing in greater or less degree if he wishes to clinch his expression with any depth of significance." [10] The search is for that quality of the imagination which Coleridge called "esemplastic," the fiber which binds objects and events together into form and shape. "Thus a poem is tough by no quality it borrows from a logical recital of events nor from the events themselves but solely from that attenuated power which draws perhaps many broken things into a dance giving them thus a full being" (SE, 14). The search for this power of association and

---

[10] William Carlos Williams, "How to Write," reprinted in *The Poems of William Carlos Williams: A Critical Study,* by Linda Welshimer Wagner (Middletown, Connecticut: Wesleyan University Press, 1964), p. 146.

orchestration takes the poet beneath the surface of consciousness toward a new "ground." And yet Williams is never a completely passive or "automatic" writer; the very construction of the "Improvisations" suggests his constant tension between the daemonic subterranean pressures and the "masculine" formative principle which seeks to explore and organize. As he tells us in *I Wanted to Write a Poem,* the project was to write for a year *something* every evening before he went to bed: "Even if I had nothing in mind at all I put something down, and as might be expected, some of the entries were pure nonsense. . . ." (IWWP, 27) What appeared at the surface had to be winnowed and many entries were discarded, while others received an interpretative "frame"—the statements at the bottom of the page which attempt to explain the Sybilline "improvisations." Not without a pedantic smile, Williams adds that he borrowed the device of placing interpretations beneath "material" from a book Pound had left in the house, the *Varie Poesie* of Pietro Metastasio (Venice, 1795). As the poet's own cover design (of ovum and circumambient spermatozoa) implies, it was a book of beginnings, many of them false starts.

The second step in the transition records more clearly Williams' life-long preoccupation with submitting every new experience to the mastery of form. *Spring and All* retains what the poet calls "surreal" prose passages, which are in fact dense but acute observations on his own poetic activity. But now he has begun to separate out and to shape the poems which have successfully sprung from the "underworld" of the emotions. On page eleven, after some virtuoso work in prose which heralds the approach of spring and concludes "THE WORLD IS NEW," he prints the first return to verse, and the justly famous "By the road to the contagious hospital." Here, in the quickening rhythms and the stark juxtaposition of barren landscape and emergent weeds, he enacts the violence and excitement of birth:

> All along the road the reddish
> purplish, forked, upstanding, twiggy
> stuff of bushes and small trees
> with dead, brown leaves under them   (SA, 12)

The entrance into this world is naked and cold, in the embrace of a "familiar" wind; but the determined life grips and stirs the soil, and stirs the feelings of the poet, at the very boundary of spring:

> Now the grass, tomorrow
> the stiff curl of wildcarrot leaf

> One by one objects are defined—
> It quickens: clarity, outline of leaf   (SA, 12)

The referent of "it," which has troubled some readers, is the vital, mobile element, the spring which quickens the landscape and the reviving imagination which quickens the poet. (Many of the "modern" aspects of Williams' poetry are sharply defined by even a casual comparison of this poem with the "Dejection Ode.")

The second poem in *Spring and All* follows immediately after. In its profusion of contending colors—a pot of gay flowers—it might represent the second half of the title. In contrast with the starkness of the first poem, it is alive with color, shape, and interpenetrating light. Persephone has reclaimed her kingdom.

It is the third poem, some pages later, which most clearly shows the artist himself after his successful passage, "The farmer in deep thought." All of the essential elements of Williams' cosmology and poetics are present here among the "blank fields": the formless earth, the harvest of forms (as yet planted only in the farmer's head), and life-giving force represented by the rain and the farmer's "composing" imagination (SA, 16-17). The moment is that one so dear to Williams, March, when life is only just beginning to stir. "The artist figure of/the farmer" is at once solid image in the composition and the emblem of the new dimension which Williams' passage had opened: a mind which is beginning to stir with the blessed rage for order. He is the "antagonist," one who contends in an athletic struggle for mastery, whether of the chaos without or the chaos within.

In the American Grain (1925) records another rite of passage which opens a new dimension in Williams' experience. Again, paradoxically, it seems to suggest an abandonment of the field of immediate experience for the self-renunciation of the historian. The poet and his wife had immersed themselves in documents—the journal of Columbus, a Norse saga, the records of the Salem witchcraft trials, the writings of Cotton Mather, Franklin, Hamilton, and John Paul Jones. But it would be a radical mistake to regard the book as an interpretation of history. As Louis Martz has justly observed, *In the American Grain* is an intensely personal examination and manifesto, "a search in the memory of America to discover, to invent, symbols of the ideals from which Williams' life and writings have developed." [11] Just as he transforms the prose styles of his sources into remarkably original constructions of his

[11] Louis Martz, "The Unicorn in Paterson: William Carlos Williams," *Thought*, XXXV (Winter 1960), 545.

own, Williams ransacks the past of his New World for exemplary figures and gestures to confirm his own sense of the human environment. What appears to be a descent into the nation's historic past is a much more willful plunge into his own memory for heroes of "the animate touch," for a significant counter to the present inhuman withdrawal from experience which he sees as the Puritan inheritance. The records are themselves a river which flows to the poet's present; as he says of the generous spirit of Père Sebastian Rasles alive in the Maine wilderness: "Reading his letters, it is a river which brings sweet water to us. *This* is a native moral source not reckoned with, peculiarly sensitive and daring in its close embrace of native things" (IAG, 120-21). Through the example of the priest, Williams is able to ascend upstream from that "vilest swillhole in Christendom, the Passaic River" for refreshment (IAG, 195). This search for a possible beginning parallels the plunge of "The Wanderer" and the descent of *Kora in Hell*. For it is the example of Daniel Boone which carries him back to earth for that periodic renewal (which Van Gennep sees as characteristic of all rites of passage). Boone is still alive for Williams "because of a descent to the ground of his desire" in the immense profusion of the wilderness:

> Boone's genius was to recognize the difficulty as neither material nor political but one purely moral and aesthetic. Filled with the wild beauty of the New World to overbrimming so long as he had what he desired, to bathe in, to explore always more deeply, to see, to feel, to touch—his instincts were contented.   (IAG, 136)

Immersion, then, in the waters of the "American experience" brings no loss of self, but rather an affirmation of a larger role for the poet as the moral force embracing his green New World, a new beginning.

After none of these critical adventures of passage is it ever possible for Williams to turn back, to refuse even briefly the new incorporation. But the rites which follow the first four lead him further in the direction of understanding and affirming the experience of human community. He explores this new solidarity in a number of ways, not always at first successfully: in the raw artifacts of the city, its signs, slogans, and the fresh anarchy of speech; in the lives of artists he has known or admired, D. H. Lawrence, Charles Demuth, Albert Einstein; in the anecdotal encounters with courage or beauty in the responses of his patients and neighbors. The efforts and indirections all point toward an attempt to enter and comprehend the notion of the *city of man*. The titles

alone of his collections during the 1930s suggest this preoccupa-
tion: *An Early Martyr and Other Poems* (the title poem is for the
young radical John Coffey), "An Elegy for D. H. Lawrence," *Adam
and Eve and the City*, "The Crimson Cyclamen" (To the Memory
of Charles Demuth). And much of his best work went into the short
stories of the depression years, *Life Along the Passaic River* and
The Knife of the Times. But for all the occasional triumphs, many
of the poems of this period reflect his growing frustration and bit-
terness at what he sees as man's inhumanity to man. For an
achieved possession of the city, its speech, and its people, Williams
had to enter again that filthy river which gives life to *Paterson*.
Although the building of the four books which form the integral
part of *Paterson* was literally the work of a lifetime, the crisis was
reached when he could see the total design of a work which was
at once a man, a river, a city, and a poem. The moment when
Williams could at last achieve this vision of solidarity and the new
structural and technical means of expressing it occurred in the
1940s. Characteristically, the vision took the form of a new incor-
poration into the life of the language about him. The problem of
the fallen city of industrial squalor became for Williams a failure
of communication between men; the "divorce" of language from
reality could only be resolved in a new "marriage" of urban man
to what he called "a redeeming language" that would repair,
rescue, and complete the human environment.

Although this immersion in the native idiom which he sought
to discover and invent led to years of experiment in prosody, to
an increasing reliance on "structural" juxtapositions of prose and
verse, to a general movement away from substantive toward kinetic
syntax, the ritual entry into the new world can be marked by the
publication, in 1944, of a small volume called *The Wedge*. Speak-
ing of it, the poet said: "I have always been proud of this book.
The Introduction, written in the most forthright prose, is an ex-
planation of my poetic creed at that time—for all time as far as
that goes." (IWWP, 70) In this introduction the poet rejects what
he takes to be the Freudian notion of the work of art as "a resort
from frustration." He sees it as an *act* of making:

> There is no poetry of distinction without formal invention, for it
> is in the intimate form that works of art achieve their exact meaning,
> in which they most resemble the machine, to give language its highest
> dignity, its illumination in the environment to which it is native.
> Such war, as the arts live and breathe by, is continuous.   (SE, 257)

The familiar figure of the artist as antagonist, composing and con-

structing, is clearly defined. But the introduction and the poems
which follow declare the intimate relation between this war and a
new kind of love which is gentle as well as violent, which can recon-
cile as well as compose. Thus, in the first poem he undertakes

> —through metaphor to reconcile
> the people and the stones.
> Compose. (No ideas
> but in things) Invent!
> Saxifrage is my flower that splits
> the rocks.   (CLP, 7)

The collection is a genuine transition, a point of departure for the
achievements of the later poetry. Just as "Paterson: the Falls" em-
bodies his program for the epic poem, and "The Dance" records
the first of the measures he will strike from Brueghel's genius, so
"To All Gentleness" and "Raleigh Was Right" reveal the poet's
immersion in a new experience of human love which is no longer
simply volcanic (like "Catastrophic Birth") and which admits of
receiving as well as giving. This vision of love governs the poems
which follow *The Wedge* and leads to the last and perhaps great-
est of Williams' rites of passage, "Asphodel, That Greeny Flower."
Love, which opens flower-like in his hand, is the only cure for a
world filled with murderers whom we must imitate

> . . . unless
> we learn from that to avoid
> being as they are, how love
> will rise out of its ashes if
> we water it, tie up the slender
> stem and keep the image of its
> lively flower chiseled upon our minds.   (CLP, 19)

The "country" without this flower will no longer bring us peace.
The landscape must be inhabited by human affection: "Love itself
a flower/with roots in a parched ground" (CLP, 52).

Study of "Philomena Andronico"

by Karl Shapiro

The following poem has never appeared in a book,[1] and I assume it is the poet's purpose to leave it only for a study of this kind. Its worksheets consist of fifteen typed pages corrected in pencil; they present, in all, five versions. As a discarded William Carlos Williams piece, I think nevertheless that it throws some light on his *pratique* as well as on his particular poetic aims. In Williams, as in Wallace Stevens to a lesser extent, we have the ultimate development of form that seeks to arrest or still the image. This is not to say that motion and action are dispensed with in this method, but that, even when the subject matter is of a very violent nature, as is often the case with Williams, the extreme surface of the poem remains or attempts to remain at a dead calm. It is a poetry as closely allied to painting as any I know.

Readers who sometimes search for the logical word sequence in

[1] The poem was later included by Williams in the first edition of *The Collected Later Poems of William Carlos Williams* (Norfolk, Connecticut: New Directions Publishing Corporation, 1950), pp. 120, 121. The reader may wish to compare the version there or in the 1963 edition of *The Collected Later Poems* with the manuscript version and variants Karl Shapiro gives. There are a number of alterations, but the final stanzas are most significantly revised. The changes seem to be made so that the movement of the words and the pauses between the lines will match more exactly the slow grace of the girl's gestures:

> in the warm still
> air lets
> her arms
> > Fall
>
> Fall
> loosely
> (waiting)
> at her sides
> > [ED.]

Williams are baffled at what seems a jumble of things set down without normal language relationships. What is good to remember in reading Williams is that the words, or at least the key words, are very like ideographs, or symbols of the objects thought of. Ordinarily we do not call to mind the object or attribute for which a word stands; the word itself is enough to satisfy our desire for a meaning. In Williams the objects themselves all but spring up before our eyes, and it is the logic of these almost-objects in careful arrangement that provides the narrative of ideas.

The poem is named "Philomena Andronico," and from the context we learn that a little (immigrant?) girl is bouncing a ball. That is all the subject matter we have. Here is what seems to be the penultimate version of the manuscript:*

> With the boys busy
> at ball
> in the worn lot
> nearby
>
> She stands in
> the short street
> reflectively bouncing
> the red ball
>
> Slowly
> practiced
> a little awkwardly
> throwing one leg over
>
> not as she had done
> formerly
> screaming and
> missing
>
> but slowly
> surely and then
> pausing first
> she throws the ball
>
> with a full slow
> very slow
> and easy motion
> following through

* It is interesting to notice that in Williams a change may involve only the typographical position of a word or a phrase.

with a slow
half turn
as the ball flies
and rolls gently

at the child's feet
~~waiting beyond~~
and yet he misses
it and turns

and runs while she
slowly regains
her former
pose

                 the
then/ runs ~~her~~ fingers
of one hand
up through
her loose short hair,
~~the quickly~~

   leans   her
to draw~~s one~~ stocking
tight and then
~~the other~~
~~waiting~~

in the warm still
air

and tilts
her hip
and lets her arms
fall loosely
(waiting) at her sides

This poem, as I say, is the ABC of Williams' technique. Nothing
half so simple appears in any of his published work, most of which
is as formally complex as this is elementary. We are lucky to find
only the essentials of a Williams poem; in this case at least we are
free to discuss only the color and the development of the ideo-
graphs. The poem is a study in the control of the objects it deals
with and the deceleration of their motions.

In Draft A the word "busy" first comes under observation and is
struck out. The second draft eliminates the first stanza entirely,
only to pick it up in the third version, but without "busy" again.
The fourth version restores the troublesome word, and it survives
in the fifth and final forms. This particular problem is not peculiar

to Williams, however, but to all poets. It merely questions a possibly inappropriate adjective. The next problem is of a different nature.

The "meter" in a visual poem of this kind is determined by spacing and by creating a mental stop or advance with the use of the appearance of the words, their groupings. Thus Version A reads:

> She stands in
> the side street
> bouncing
>
> a red ball slowly *or* a red
>   ball slowly **a**

Version B reads:

> she stands in
> the side streets
> bouncing a red
>
> ball slowly

Version C repeats B, and D inserts a decelerating adverb:

> she stands in
> the side street
> ~~reflectively~~
> bouncing a red ball
>
> slowly

which, like "busy," is first doubted and finally accepted. The semifinal version:

> She stands in
> the short street
> reflectively/ bouncing
> a ~~the~~ red ball
>
> Slowly

introduces the further change "the short street," which again defines a space. The final draft of the manuscript:

> She stands in
> the short street
> reflectively bouncing
> the red ball
>
> Slowly

definitely fixes the pace of the poem, which nevertheless tends to speed up. The words "slow," "slowly," and "very slow" occur six times in the course of the poem. Other brakes are "reflectively," "surely," "pausing," "easy motion," "gently," "former pose," "half turn," "waiting," "still air." The word "quickly" is struck out in the semi-final draft—I should suppose quickly, were it not that it had persisted through so many versions.

Throughout the evolution of the poem as much attention is given to the spacing of unchanged words and groups of words as to the internal changes themselves. These are as varied and as numerous as occur in the worksheets of a Spender poem but are even more difficult to follow because we know so little of the medium and cannot follow the method of selection as clearly.

Certain other word configurations in the poem are extremely piquant. They seem to add another dimension to the picture, without indicating how. Philomena stands in the side street (Draft B) bouncing a red ball and hoisting one leg:

> over not as
> formerly screaming
> and missing

"Formerly" could be a moment ago (the moment before the poem) or a year ago, a recollection from the poet's past. "Screaming" (with vexation?) does not help qualify the image. The odd use of the word "yet" is another delicate reference to some hidden emotion in the observer.

> the ball flies
> and rolls
> gently at the child's
>
> feet and yet he
> misses it and

I think "yet" is intended to convey a suggestion of uneasiness and to create an interference in the reader's mind.

Judging this composition in the light of Williams' more intricate work, I think any conclusion would be risky except this. The poet's emotions, ideas, and sensations are selected and tranquilized in the eye; then distributed on paper as ideographs, and finally arranged, as an artist arranges the elements in a picture. The surface tension of this poetry is so great that it seems impossible for submerged material to break through, or for the reader to see down through the exterior.

William Carlos Williams

by Robert Lowell

Dr. Williams and his work are part of me, yet I come on them
as a critical intruder. I fear I shall spoil what I have to say, just
as I somehow got off on the wrong note about Williams with Ford
Madox Ford twenty-five years ago. Ford was wearing a stained
robin's-egg blue pajama top, reading Theocritus in Greek, and
guying me about my "butterfly existence," so removed from the
labors of a professional writer. I was saying something awkward,
green and intense in praise of Williams, and Ford, while agreeing,
managed to make me feel that I was far too provincial, genteel and
puritanical to understand what I was saying. And why not? Wasn't
I, as Ford assumed, the grandson or something of James Russell
Lowell and the cousin of Lawrence Lowell, a young man doomed to
trifle with poetry and end up as President of Harvard or ambassa-
dor to England?

I have stepped over these pitfalls. I have conquered my hereditary
disadvantages. Except for writing, nothing I've touched has shone.
When I think about writing on Dr. Williams, I feel a chaos of
thoughts and images, images cracking open to admit a thought,
thoughts dragging their roots for the soil of an image. When I
woke up this morning, something unusual for this summer was
going on!—pinpricks of rain were falling in a reliable, comforting
simmer. Our town was blanketed in the rain of rot and the rain
of renewal. New life was muscling in, everything growing moved
on its one-way trip to the ground. I could feel this, yet believe our
universal misfortune was bearable and even welcome. An image
held my mind during these moments and kept returning—an old
fashioned New England cottage freshly painted white. I saw a
shaggy, triangular shade on the house, trees, a hedge, or their
shadows, the blotch of decay. The house might have been the house

"William Carlos Williams" by Robert Lowell. Reprinted from *The Hudson
Review*, XIV (Winter 1961-62), 530-36. Copyright © 1962 by The Hudson Re-
view, Inc. Reprinted by permission of The Hudson Review, Inc.

I was now living in, but it wasn't; it came from the time when I was a child, still unable to read and living in the small town of Barnstable on Cape Cod. Inside the house was a birdbook with an old stiff and steely engraving of a sharp-shinned hawk. The hawk's legs had a reddish brown buffalo fuzz on them; behind was the blue sky, bare and abstracted from the world. In the present, pinpricks of rain were falling on everything I could see, and even on the white house in my mind, but the hawk's picture, being indoors I suppose, was more or less spared. Since I saw the picture of the hawk, the pinpricks of rain have gone on, half the people I once knew are dead, half the people I now know were then unborn, and I have learned to read.

An image of a white house with a blotch on it—this is perhaps the start of a Williams poem. If I held this image closely and honestly enough, the stabbing detail might come and with it the universal that belonged to this detail and nowhere else. Much wrapping would have to be cut away, and many elegiac cadences with their worn eloquence and loftiness. This is how I would like to write about Dr. Williams. I would collect impressions, stare them into rightness, and let my mind-work and judgments come as they might naturally.

When I was a freshman at Harvard, nothing hit me so hard as the Norton Lectures given by Robert Frost. Frost's revolutionary power, however, was not in his followers, nor in the student literary magazine, the *Advocate,* whose editor had just written a piece on speech rhythms in the "Hired Man," a much less up-to-date thing to do then than now. Our only strong and avant-garde man was James Laughlin. He was much taller and older than we were. He knew Henry Miller, and exotic young American poetesses in Paris, spent summers at Rapallo with Ezra Pound, and was getting out the first number of his experimental annual, *New Directions.* He knew the great, and he himself wrote deliberately flat descriptive and anecdotal poems. We were sarcastic about them, but they made us feel secretly that we didn't know what was up in poetry. They used no punctuation or capitals, and their only rule was that each line should be eleven or fifteen typewriter spaces long. The author explained that this metric was "as rational as any other" and was based on the practice of W. C. Williams, a poet and pediatrician living in Rutherford, New Jersey. About this time, Laughlin published a review somewhere, perhaps even in the *Harvard Advocate,* of Williams' last small volume. In it, he pushed the metric of typewriter spaces, and quoted from a poem, "The Catholic Bells," to show Williams' "mature style at fifty!" This was a memorable phrase, and one that made maturity seem possible, but a long way off. I more or less memorized "The Catholic Bells," and spent months trying to console myself by detecting immaturities in whatever Williams had written before he was fifty.

The Catholic Bells

Tho' I'm no Catholic
I listen hard when the bells
in the yellow-brick tower
of their new church

ring down the leaves
ring in the frost upon them
and the death of the flowers
ring out the grackle

toward the south, the sky
darkened by them, ring in
the new baby of Mr. and Mrs.
Krantz which cannot

for the fat of its cheeks
open well its eyes . . .

What I liked about "The Catholic Bells" were the irrelevant associations I hung on the words "frost" and "Catholic," and still more its misleading similarity to the "Ring out wild bells" section of *In Memoriam*. Other things upset and fascinated me and made me feel I was in a world I would never quite understand. Were the spelling "Tho,'" strange in a realistic writer, and the iambic rhythm of the first seven words part of some inevitable sound pattern? I had dipped into Edith Sitwell's criticism and was full of inevitable sound patterns. I was sure that somewhere hidden was a key that would make this poem as regular as the regular meters of Tennyson. There had to be something outside the poem I could hang onto because what was inside dizzied me! the shocking scramble of the august and the crass in making the Catholic church "new" and "yellow-brick," the cherubic ugliness of the baby, belonging rather horribly to "Mr. and Mrs./Krantz," and seen by the experienced, mature pediatrician as unable to see "for the fat of its cheeks"—this last a cunning shift into anapests. I was surprised that Williams used commas, and that my three or four methods of adjusting his lines to uniform typewriter spaces failed. I supposed he had gone on to some bolder and still more mature system.

To explain the full punishment I felt on first reading Williams,

I should say a little about what I was studying at the time. A year or so before, I had read some introductory books on the enjoyment of poetry, and was knocked over by the examples in the free verse sections. When I arrived at college, independent, fearful of advice and with all the world before me, I began to rummage through the Cambridge bookshops. I found books that must have been looking for a buyer since the student days of Trumbull Stickney: soiled metrical treatises written by obscure English professors in the eighteen-nineties. They were full of glorious things: rising rhythm, falling rhythm, feet with Greek names, stanzas from Longfellow's *Psalm of Life,* John Drinkwater and Swinburne. Nothing seemed simpler than meter. I began experiments with an exotic foot, short, long, two shorts, then fell back on iambics. My material now took twice as many words, and I rolled out Spenserian stanzas on Job and Jonah surrounded by recently seen Nantucket scenery. Everything I did was grand, ungrammatical and had a timeless, hackneyed quality. All this was ended by reading Williams. It was as through some homemade ship, part Spanish galleon, part paddlewheels, kitchen pots and elastic bands and worked by hand, had anchored to a filling station.

In the "Catholic Bells," the joining of religion and non-religion, of piety and a hard, nervous secular knowingness are typical of Williams. Further along in this poem, there is a piece of mere description that has always stuck in my mind.

                              (the

          grapes still hanging to
          the vines along the nearby
          Concordia Halle like broken
          teeth in the head of an

          old man)

Take out the Concordia Halle and the grape vines crackle in the wind with a sour, impoverished dryness; take out the vines and the Concordia Halle has lost its world. Williams has pages and pages of description that are as good as this. It is his equivalent of, say, the Miltonic sentence, the dazzling staple and excellence which he can always produce. Williams has said that he uses the forms he does for quick changes of tone, atmosphere and speed. This makes him dangerous and difficult to imitate, because most poets have little change of tone, atmosphere and speed in them.

I have emphasized Williams' simplicity and nakedness and have no doubt been misleading. His idiom comes from many sources, from speech and reading, both of various kinds; the blend, which is his own invention, is generous and even exotic. Few poets can come near to his wide clarity and dashing rightness with words, his dignity and almost Alexandrian modulations of voice. His short lines often speed up and simplify hugely drawn out and ornate sentence structures. I once typed out his direct but densely observed poem, "The Semblables," in a single prose paragraph. Not a word or its placing had been changed, but the poem had changed into a piece of smothering, magnificent rhetoric, much more like Faulkner than the original Williams.

The difficulties I found in Williams twenty-five years ago are still difficulties for me. Williams enters me, but I cannot enter him. Of course, one cannot catch any good writer's voice or breathe his air. But there's something more. It's as if no poet except Williams had really seen America or heard its language. Or rather, he sees and hears what we all see and hear and what is most obvious, but no one else has found this a help or an inspiration. This may come naturally to Dr. Williams from his character, surroundings and occupation. I can see him rushing from his practice to his type-writer, happy that so much of the world has rubbed off on him, maddened by its hurry. Perhaps he had no choice. Anyway, what others have spent lifetimes in building up personal styles to gather what has been snatched up on the run by Dr. Williams? When I say that I cannot enter him, I am almost saying that I cannot enter America. This troubles me. I am not satisfied to let it be. Like others I have picked up things here and there from Williams, but this only makes me marvel all the more at his unique and searing journey. It is a Dantesque journey, for he loves America excessively, as if it were *the* truth and *the* subject; his exasperation is also excessive, as if there were no other hell. His flowers rustle by the superhighways and pick up all our voices.

A seemingly unending war has been going on for as long as I can remember between Williams and his disciples and the principals and disciples of another school of modern poetry. The "beats" are on one side, the university poets are on the other. Lately the gunfire has been hot. With such unlikely Williams recruits as Karl Shapiro blasting away, it has become unpleasant to stand in the middle in a position of impartiality.

The war is an old one for me. In the late Thirties, I was at Kenyon College to study under John Crowe Ransom. The times hummed with catastrophe and ideological violence, both political and aesthetical. The English departments were clogged with worthy, but outworn and backward-looking scholars, whose tastes in the moderns were most often superficial, random and vulgar. Students who wanted to write got little practical help from their professors. They studied the classics as monsters that were slowly losing their fur and feathers and leaking a little sawdust. What one did one's self was all chance and shallowness, and no profession seemed wispier and less needed than that of the poet. My own group, that of Tate and Ransom, was all for the high discipline, for putting on the full armor of the past, for making poetry something that would take a man's full weight and that would bear his complete intelligence, passion and subtlety. Almost anything, the Greek and Roman classics, Elizabethan dramatic poetry, 17th century metaphysical verse, old and modern critics, aestheticians and philosophers, could be suppled up and again made necessary. The struggle perhaps centered on making the old metrical forms usable again to express the depths of one's experience.

For us Williams was of course part of the revolution that had renewed poetry, but he was a byline. Opinions varied on his work. It was something fresh, secondary and minor, or it was the best that free verse could do. He was the one writer with the substance, daring and staying power to make the short free verse poem something considerable. One was shaken when the radical conversative critic, Yvor Winters, spoke of Williams' "By the road to the contagious hospital" as a finer, more lasting piece of craftsmanship than "Gerontion."

Well, nothing will do for everyone. It's hard for me to see how I and the younger poets I was close to could at that time have learned much from Williams. It was all we could do to keep alive and follow our own heavy program. That time is gone, and now young poets are perhaps more conscious of the burden and the hardening of this old formalism. Too many poems have been written to rule. They show off their authors' efforts and mind, but little more. Often the culture seems to have passed them by. And once more, Dr. Williams is a model and a liberator. What will come, I don't know. Williams, unlike, say, Marianne Moore, seems to be one of those poets who can be imitated anonymously. His style is almost a common style and even what he claims for it— *the American style*. Somehow, written without his speed and genius, the results are usually dull, a poem at best well-made but without breath.

Williams is part of the great breath of our literature. *Paterson* is our *Leaves of Grass*. The times have changed. A drastic experimental art is now expected and demanded. The scene is dense with the dirt and power of industrial society. Williams looks on it with exasperation, terror and a kind of love. His short poems are singularly perfect thrusts, maybe the best that will ever be written of their kind, because neither the man nor the pressure will be found again. When I think of his last longish autobiographical poems, I remember his last reading I heard. It was at Wellesley. I think about three thousand students attended. It couldn't have been more crowded in the wide-galleried hall and I had to sit in the aisle. The poet appeared, one whole side partly paralysed, his voice just audible, and here and there a word misread. No one stirred. In the silence he read his great poem, "Of Asphodel, That Greeny Flower," a triumph of simple confession—somehow he delivered to us what was impossible, something that **was** both poetry and beyond poetry.

I think of going with Dr. Williams and his son to visit his mother, very old, almost a hundred, and unknowing, her black eyes boring through. And Williams saying to her, "Which would you rather see, us, or three beautiful blonds?" As we left, he said, "The old bitch will live on but I may die tomorrow!" You could not feel shocked. Few men had felt and respected anyone more than Williams had his old mother. And in seeing him out strolling on a Sunday after a heart attack: the town seemed to know him and love him and take him in its stride, as we will do with his great pouring of books, his part in the air we breathe and will breathe.

A Character For Love[1]

by Robert Creeley

We can hope that the woman be merciful, a kind of repose (and our rejection in part) for that for which she attacks. And yet there is no woman either to be kind or to live with a kind man, and rightly. The man who would come to her comes with his own weapons, and if he is not a fool, he uses them.

That much might well be dogma—an apology only to those who have gone down before its alternative, the 'understanding.' It was this that Lawrence fought all his life, perhaps more closely (more desperately) than any man before or since. Because we can have no way to declare love, except by the act of it.

Here[2] it is that Dr. Williams not so much rests as still persists— in that persistence, which, because it knows itself (and will *not* understand), is love too.

> There are men
> who as they live
> fling caution to the

"A Character For Love" by Robert Creeley. From *Black Mountain Review*, I (Summer 1954), 45-48. Reprinted by permission of Robert Creeley.

[1] In a letter to Robert Creeley, August 9, 1954, Williams wrote as follows about this essay: "But the part of your letter which most interested me was, I hope I will be forgiven, that which was directed to my own poems. The enclosure was I take it from a notice which is to appear in your magazine at some future time. It is very interesting to me because of its theme: woman. I have never come down as hard on that as I would like to or, better put, as I have dared to. Yet what you have seen and assembled under one head is for that all the more forceful. I don't mean to say that as with the sailor who probes his harpoon into the whale's side the whole sea will ultimately be red stained. In any case, your letter impressed me . . ." (This passage, hitherto unpublished, is printed here with the kind permission of Robert Creeley and Mrs. Florence H. Williams.)

[2] William Carlos Williams, *The Desert Music* (New York: Random House, 1954).

160

> wind and women praise them
> > and love them for it.
> > > Cruel as the claws of
>
> a cat . .

You do not describe this thing, neither you nor I. Married, the world becomes that act, or nothing.

> The female principle of the world
> > is my appeal
> > > in the extremity
> to which I have come.

I think that much of this content (by no means to beg it) came from him from the first, and, to that extent, American poetry had something even Poe (whom Williams alone saw this in) could not in his own dilemma give it. It is interesting, certainly that, to read the last part of the Poe essay in *In The American Grain*—where Poe's attempt to register himself is so characterized as this persistence, this hammering at the final edge of contact.

And this is the same force of Williams' stories, the best of them I think, even that possible vagueness in the one about the returning doctor, at the friend's house (also a doctor), and of the friend's wife who comes in and sits there, in the dark, by the edge of the bed, lies down on it, because *he* cannot sleep.

> > > You are a woman and
> > it was
> > > a woman's gesture.
>
> . . . .
> > > I declare it boldly
> > with my heart
> > > in my teeth
> > > > and my knees knocking
> > together. Yet I declare
> > > it, and by God's word
> > > > It is no lie.

The *Autobiography,* more than any of his other books, now, is the place where the materials of his work are given—not done, but there to be found and related, if that is the purpose, to their forms in his art. What the poem is—beyond his sense of this service as 'capsule for punishable secrets' or including it—comes again and again to the fact of women. In the preface to the book he speaks

of that 'form' which men have given to his life, but it is women
who have made for the 'energy'. And energy begins it.

> Of asphodel, that greeny flower,
>   like a buttercup
>   upon its branching stem—
> save that it's green and wooden—
>   I come, my sweet,
>   to sing to you.

For what reason, to sing, even to be a 'poet'?

>   I *am* a poet! I
>   am. I am. I am a poet, I reaffirmed, ashamed

> Now the music volleys through as in
> a lonely moment I hear it.   Now it is all
> about me. The dance! The verb detaches itself
> seeking to become articulate   .

There shall be no other judge—*not* judge, but she who will take
it. And for that reason, that it begins where all things (*mind you*)
begin, the dance is the plain fact of contact, god help us.

>   You seem quite normal. Can you tell me? Why
>   does one want to write a poem?

>   Because it's there to be written.

>   Oh. A matter of inspiration then?

>   Of necessity.

>   Oh. But what sets it off?

>   I am that he whose brains
>   are scattered
>   aimlessly

At this point one turns, to laugh (ha), because it is what you
wanted? Well, put it that here we are thrown out, not by Williams
but by that which he knows, perfectly. We shall get no thanks for
what we do, 'poets' or not. Nor can we lie down, asking it.

>   There is, in short,
>   a counter stress,
>   born of the sexual shock,
>   which survives it

consonant with the moon,
to keep its own mind.

We have had so much hope, both in love and in poetry, that I wonder what is or can be left. Yet put them together and you will have nothing at all. You cannot sit in a woman's lap, however comfortable. And, despite the humiliation, the door must be shut of necessity—until you can bang it down or open it.

You understand
I had to meet you
after the event
and have still to meet you.
Love
to which you too shall bow
along with me—
a flower
a weakest flower
shall be our trust
and not because
we are too feeble
to do otherwise
but because
at the height of my power
I risked what I had to do,
therefore to prove
that we love each other
while my very bones sweated
that I could not cry out to you
in the act.

Let men do what they will, generally—there will be no statement beyond this. It is fantastic, to me, that Williams at such a time as now confronts him should be so incredibly clear. Yet, what else to be.

Hear me out
for I too am concerned
and every man
who wants to die at peace in his bed
besides.

The Farmer's Daughters:
A True Story about People

by Cid Corman

Bill was upstairs. (I was visiting 9 Ridge Road, 1954.) Floss was explaining his nervousness whenever the phone rang. He thinks it's for him, a patient. Few seem to realize that 70% of his life has been given to his practice.

She was implying, perhaps, that writing occupied only part of the remaining 30%. But life, like death, has a funny way of getting round percentages. And to read these stories,[1] without exception relating, directly or indirectly, to his work as a G.P. in and out of his office (at home) in Rutherford, New Jersey, is to realize rather that writing of this order is an extension, not an escape or evasion or diminution, of a man's days and nights.

These sketches, "verbal transcriptions," histories, anecdotes, tales, are all instances of one man's remarkable capacity for love. Love of people, foremost, but no less—with enduring respect—a love of human expressiveness, of language, particular speech, its trickiness, vivacity, penetration.

If I had to choose which, of all the "pieces," I preferred most, I suppose I'd say: "Old Doc Rivers," for its groping toward understanding, the openness and clarity of its relations, the way the local is a universe and is again itself; "The Use of Force," for all its anthologizing, a beautiful clean thing, prose, direct in its attack, sure in its sense of when to leave off, its language crisp and true, touching; and "The Farmers' Daughters," perhaps the most ambitious work, with its broken chronology, weaving incident and

"*The Farmers' Daughters:* A True Story about People." From *The Massachusetts Review*, III (1962), 319-24. Copyright © 1962, by the Massachusetts Review, Inc. Reprinted by permission of The Massachusetts Review.

[1] *The Farmers' Daughters: The Collected Stories of William Carlos Williams* (New York: New Directions Publishing Corporation, 1961).

anecdote, perception and experience, with honest feeling, words falling for words, free and fluent and with complete control.

In some of the earliest pieces I have gritted my teeth at the too heavy sense of the "dialect." The writer seems too much "outside" and making a thing up, not wholly with it, *not* recounting it, trying too hard to impress. The commitment uncertain, off. But with "Mind and Body" the inside opens:

> . . . I know people think I am a nut. I was an epileptic as a child. I know I am a manic depressive. But doctors are mostly fools. . . .

(I begin to hear the voice of a "later" poet, Robert Creeley, foreshadowed.)

How often, as here, the good doctor tries to project a woman's sense of things, her involvement in body, person, place, in things and in "relations." "It is life, what we see and decide for ourselves, that counts."

For response to and a gathering-up of language, in the same story, consider this:

> . . . When I was talking to the Jesuit, who came to teach me what the church meant, I told him I could not believe that. He said, I should. I asked him, Do you? But he did not answer me. . . .

Set this against Charles Olson's "Pastoral Letter" in his recent *Maximus Poems,* if you want to see evidence of what Dr. Williams has quietly effected "in the art":

> . . . "I don't believe
> I know your name." Given.
> How do you do,
> how do you do. And then:
> "Pardon me, but
> what church
> do you belong to,
> may I ask?"
> . . . .
> I sd, you may, sir.
> He sd, what, sir.
> I sd, none,
> sir. . . .

The short punched-out speech, sporadic, laconic, easy, but not facile, straight-on. Not exaggerated, for the true is crazy enough and hard enough to hang on to. And as he gradually works his way

open, into the open, he is what he is, William Carlos Williams, half
Spanish, half English, part Jewish, part this and part that, man
and woman, Pater-son, make no mistake, "Doc," and his wife is
Floss, and there are the two boys, and there is the neighborhood.
And Rutherford-Paterson opens to contain and be contained to
brimming. As a flower in fertile soil. Red roses or "white weeds."
Jonquils that "want affection," love, and raspberries, as one learns,
to be picked from a roadside and brought "home" to share.

But is it "art"? The question *is* asked, in and out of school. Sadly.
For to express relation with feeling this cleanly, this precisely, with-
out any phoney theatricalism, without resorting to a pompous
rhetoric, or a desire to overwhelm with literary machinery, if art
is anything, is what this is. There is a glory in people, his glory (as
well as ours), the stuff they are made of, we are, stubbornness, in-
domitability, even within the confines of ignorance, stupidity, pov-
erty. "He was liked," would be the simplest comment one would ex-
pect his townsfolk to say, if asked about him. How could he not be?
Concerned about payment, on a visit at whatever hour, but not
overly concerned, willing to do it for "nothing," for a laugh or a
lark sometimes, for a word or a gesture, a look, for the love of it,
for the love of them. For the Polish mother who smiled when she
lost her "first daughter" at birth, for the Italian peasant who paid
him in snuff. For the love of Mike, sentimental! How, if the feeling
is accurate. He is guilty and proud, moved and obdurate, sensible
and sensitive. "I have found . . . that we must live for others, that
we are not alone in the world and we cannot live alone."

". . . What was he going to do? How did he know? Where was
he going to stay when it got cold? Whose the hell's business was
that? What would he eat? Beans and bananas, chewing gum, caviar
and roast duck. With that she left him. And later on it grew
cold. . . ." A love for the weak and the strong, respect for the off-
beat, for the independent soul, for dignity, for sheer doggedness
and spite, for a thin body holding out for life, for candor, for gen-
erosity, for care.

Do they get "under"? Does anything that is not there? The ma-
jority of these recountings, if not all of them, strike me as probably
having been written "at the moment," at the spur; they are so close
to event. Yet, as often as not, there is a "history" involved and I
see that much more goes on here than meets the eye: a world, inside.
The cadences of speech, the speed and the relaxation, the deftness
and alertness of ear and mind, bespeak authority.

In "Old Doc Rivers" he can attack and defend at the same time,
and he mutes verdicts:

Well, Mary, what is it?

I have a pain in my side, doctor.

How long have you had it, Mary?

Today, doctor. It's the first time.

Just today.

Yes, doctor.

Climb up on the table. Pull up your dress. Throw that sheet over you.
Come on, come on. Up with you. Come on now, Mary. Pull up your knees.

Oooh!

He could be cruel and crude. And like all who are so, he could be
sentimentally tender also, and painstaking without measure. . . .

As against practitioners of the "tough guy" school, like Heming-
way, say, his language is at once more convincing and accurate, and
out of the body, out of the mouth, less manufactured, less "literary."
And yet not at all unaware of the problems of what goes, what
sticks. He had written, as early as 1932, answering academicism and
snobbery:

> . . . I cannot swallow the half-alive poetry which knows nothing of
> totality. . . . Nothing is beyond poetry. It is the one solid element
> on which our lives can rely, the "word" of so many disguises, includ-
> ing as it does man's full consciousness, high and low, in living objec-
> tivity. . . . It is, in its rare major form, a world in fact come to ar-
> rest of self realization: that eternity of the present which most stum-
> ble over in seeking—or drug themselves into littleness to attain. . . .

The vision, no matter the structure of prose, is a poet's, making
poets of us too. Each relation relates one to another. I think any
reader will find a coherence; they are all "of a piece." And the
"form"? The living speech of a time, a place, a people. All elements
of society come to his feast: children, adults, old folk, animals,
Polacks, Wops, Jews, the Irish and Scotch and English, the south-
erner, the Negro, lady and bum, the wise guy and the tease, the
professional and the conversationalist. William Carlos Williams. It
may be that I recognize a world my own and so feel "at home" and
drawn to it. But there's also "more."

It has to do with a man's zest, his brio, his appetite for life, his
disgust, or the confrontation of death, an eagerness for detail, a
nose, an ear, an unfailing willingness, desire, to know and know
more, to encounter "them." He doesn't blink at what he sees either.
On the contrary, what he sees is what makes him want to see more,
to speak to a "patient" always as a person, as this man or this
woman or this child and no other. He makes me want to address

my world, wherever I touch it, with equal frankness and affection.
Unblinking. Perceiving.

"Down to earth," I'd say. American archaeology, as a friend
where I now am staying might say. Not the classical bit of fancy
goods and dream boats, but the bones, the beads, the chipping
stones, flints, arrowheads, artifacts of a difficult and often bare
existence, a raw country building. Silver dollars on a skeleton's
eye sockets. Money plastered everywhere. Seen. Faced. Not pan-
dered to or for. A knowledge, I'd say, that the most beautiful vases
are also made of clay. He makes the pot and paints it, with earth's
colors.

And no slouch is he as a weaver, out of the so-called "common"
thread—to show us, we onlookers, how uncommon our lives may be
and often are, as in "The Farmers' Daughters," where he moderates
lovingly between two women he knew professionally and as friends,
throughout a long career, the very image of his career, the poetry of
their lives touching his, or his touch lifting them into a world of
poetry, a world where what is true shines.

His order is that of disorder, but sensed, grasped, embraced,
danced with, released. He says it himself, as of a house of an ad-
mired patient:

> . . . I have seldom seen such disorder and brokenness—such a mass
> of unrelated parts of things lying about. That's it! I concluded to
> myself. An unrecognizable order! Actually—the new! And so good-
> natured and calm. So definitely the thing! And so compact. Excellent.
> And with such patina of use. Everything definitely "painty" . . .

"I'm struck by his honesty and concern, the openness of both."

These are love stories, all, and one of the quietest of them,
"Country Rain," speaks for both himself and Floss of their relation
and our relation to them, to others. It opens towards the request
for it ("commissioned" by the heart):

> If this were Switzerland, I thought, we'd call it lovely: wisps of low
> cloud rising slowly among the heavily wooded hills. But since it's
> America we call it simply wet. Wet and someone at another of the
> tables asks if it's going to stop raining or keep it up all day. . . .

To write as simply and fluently and perceptively as that may suggest
to some that it's "easy." Don't you believe it. It takes years of listen-
ing, of speaking well, of caring to. It requires the mind of a poet.

Perhaps this is more obvious, or will be, in this quote from the
end of the same piece. He and Floss, on a wet summer morning
gone to pick up the mail for the country house where they are vaca-

tioning, find they have "time" and drive on into the old landscape, discussing some of the people they have recently met.

I stopped the car in a dark, heavily wooded portion of the road dripping with the rain from the overhanging spruces. Floss looked at me. There was a sharp drop to the left beyond the half-rotten section of a crude guard rail where in the intense silence a small stream could be heard talking to itself among the stones.

What are you stopping here for?

I want to look at a rock. As I spoke I backed the car about twenty feet, drew in toward the embankment and shut off the engine.

The rock lay at about eye level close to my side of the road, the upper surface of it sloping slightly toward me with the hillside. Not a very big rock. What had stopped me was the shaggy covering which completely inundated it. The ferns, a cropped-short, dark-green fern, was the outstanding feature, growing thickly over an underlying cover of dense moss. But there was also a broad-leafed vine running lightly among the ferns, weaving the pattern together.

That wasn't all. The back portion of the rock, which wasn't much larger than the top of an ordinary dining-room table slightly raised at one side and a little tilted, supported both the rotten stump of a tree long since decayed but, also, a brother to that tree—coming in fact from the same root and very much alive, as big as a man's arm, a good solid arm—a ten-foot tree about whose base a small thicket of brambles clustered. Ferns of three sorts closed in from the sides completing the picture. A most ungrammatical rock.

Isn't this magnificent! Let's bring the two school teachers out here for a ride tomorrow, said Floss. They'd love it. Have you ever talked to them? she added. They're sweet.

No, I said, observing the woods ascending the hillside in the rain, but their situation among the dones, the aints and the seens amuses me. I've been wondering what they are thinking.

Don't worry, said Floss. They know what it's all about.

Look, I said, after we had rolled forward another half mile or so, do you see what I see?

Oh, said Floss, raspberries!

We stopped again, it was still raining, so I told her to stay where she was while I got down to pick some of the fruit, the remainder of what I could see had been an abundant crop recently growing at the side of the road sloping toward the stream.

Oh, taste them! said Flossie when I had brought them to her in my hand. They're dripping with juice. Anyone who would put sugar on such berries, well, would be just a barbarian. Perhaps we could stop again here tomorrow and pick enough for everybody.

A steady, heavy rain, she added. The farmers will like that. And then as an afterthought: Do you think Ruth will ever marry?

Why? I answered her.

I'd be a barbarian to add more. But I can't refrain adding a bit from the beginning of the next story "Inquest" and let that be it:

What we save, what we have, what we do. No matter. That which we most dearly cherish, *that* we shall lose, the one thing we most desire. What remains?

To be and remain interesting—with reservations—perhaps. . . .

Stories? Yes: "a world in fact come."

William Carlos Williams

by Thom Gunn

It was Eliot who dominated poetry until the early 1950s, and such is literary fashion that apparently Williams could not but suffer—being misunderstood or, more commonly, disregarded under such dominance. By all the critics who followed Eliot's lead (that is, by most critics), Williams was regarded, when he was remembered, as a kind of Menshevik, without importance. His work was unpublished and thus largely unread in England until after his death, and less than ten years ago an influential English critic could still sum it up as "William Carlos Williams' poetry of red brick houses, suburban wives, cheerful standardised interiors." America is larger than England, and thus has a little more room for variety, but there too literary opinion is centralised, and in that huge landscape Williams often went undiscerned in the 1930s and 1940s.

What must be stressed, at this late date, is that he offers a valid — alternative of style and attitude to the others available. It is offered not in his theory, which is fragmentary, sometimes inconsistent, and often poorly expressed, but in his poetry, which is among the best of our time. He is somebody from whom it is time we started taking lessons. Although he insisted on the American idiom, we must remember why: writing "thoroughly local in origin has some chance — of being universal in application"; that idiom is part of a widely-used language, his enrichment of which has a bearing on all of us who read it and write it.

The first book of his to be published over here was his most recently written, *Pictures from Brueghel*, which contains his last three collections of poems. There is a bareness about it that I can imagine was at first disconcerting to readers unfamiliar with Williams. But the bareness is not a sign of tiredness, rather it is the translation

into language of a new ease in his relationship with the external
world. A result of the ease is seen in the much greater emphasis on
the personal that we find in this volume. In "Dog Injured in the
Street" and "The Drunk and the Sailor," for example, poems which
twenty years before would merely have implied Williams as on-
looker, the subject is Williams himself so much involved in what
he witnesses that he as good as participates in it. Another result of
the ease is in the style, which is transparent to his intentions as
never before. Statement emerges from Williams as both subject and
author of the poem, not from him merely as author.

It is, however, from *Paterson* that Williams consciously dates his
final development in style. The passage from Book II that he here
reprints as a separate poem entitled "The Descent" contains many
lines divided into three parts, which he called "variable feet." I do
not find the name very clear: as Alan Stephens has pointed out in
a review, a variable foot is as meaningless a term as an elastic inch;
but if calling it so helped Williams to write this last volume, then
it is sufficiently justified. Specifically, it gave him a rationale for
the short lines grouped in threes that he wanted to use, of which
the rhythms are as flexible and varied as in the best of his earlier
poetry. This poem is about old age and is expressed largely in ab-
stract terms; in tone, even in sound, it bears an astonishing—though
we may hardly assume derivative—resemblance to some of the best
passages of the *Four Quartets*: it advances with a halting, explora-
tory movement which is itself much of the poem's meaning. He is
speaking of the re-creation achieved by memory:

> No defeat is made up entirely of defeat—since
> the world it opens is always a place
>   formerly
>   unsuspected. A
> world lost,
>   a world unsuspected,
>   beckons to new places
> and no whiteness (lost) is so white as the memory
> of whiteness .

Memory is a means of renewal, and for Williams anything that re-
news is an instrument for the exploration and definition of the new
world, which he labours both to "possess" and be part of. For pos-
session of the details is achieved not through the recording of them,
but through the record's adherence to his feeling for them. The
process is not of accumulation but of self-renewal.

the roar of the present, a speech—
is, of necessity, my sole concern .

he has said, in *Paterson*, but he is agent for the present only through the fidelity of his love for it.

The nature of the process is defined in this book with a renewed confidence, also. If in *Spring and All* the poet is seen as the firm antagonist to disorder and in *Paterson* as helplessly involved with that disorder, he is seen in "The Sparrow" finally as in a world where perhaps the words order and disorder are irrelevant. The sparrow is to a certain degree helpless, but he can "flutter his wings/in the dust" and "cry out lustily." In this poem the poet and his subject matter share in the same activity, the essence of which is the expression of delight at one's own vigour. Vigour and delight inform the style itself, relating anecdote, description and statement smoothly and easily. "It is the poem/of his existence/that triumphed/finally," he says of the sparrow, and in saying so might have been writing his own epitaph, for poem and existence are seen here to be expressed in similar terms.

There is more than self-expression involved; and, clearly, if we wish to learn from Williams' achievement, we should mark the clarity of evocation, the sensitivity of movement, and the purity of language in his efforts to realise spontaneity. But at the same time we should remember that these qualities, easy as they are to localise, cannot be learned from him in isolation. They, and the self-discipline controlling them, derive from a habitual sympathy, by which he recognises his own energy in that of the young housewife, the boys at the street corner, the half-wit girl who helps in the house, the sparrow, or the buds alternating down a bough. His stylistic qualities are governed, moreover, by a tenderness and generosity of feeling which makes them fully humane. For it is a humane action to attempt the rendering of a thing, person, or experience in the exact terms of its existence.

Chronology of Important Dates

> If number, measure, and weighing
> Be taken away from any art,
> That which remains will not be much.

1883	September 17: William Carlos Williams born in Rutherford, New Jersey, of an English father, William George Williams, and a Puerto Rican mother, Raquel Hélène (Hoheb). Early education in Rutherford schools; after completing the eighth grade he was taken abroad.
1897-99	In school at le Château de Lancy near Geneva and later briefly at the Lycée Condorcet.
1899-1902	Attends Horace Mann High School; heart murmur discovered.
1902	Admitted (by special examination) to the Medical School of the University of Pennsylvania. While studying in Philadelphia he meets Ezra Pound and through him Hilda Doolittle; long walks with Charles Demuth and work on a long Keatsian poem.
1906	Receives M.D.
1906-09	Internship at the old French Hospital and at Child's Hospital in New York City.
1909	*Poems.* Rutherford: Privately printed. 22 pp. Costs the poet "about $50.00": about four copies sold at $0.25 each. Epigraph: "Happy melodist forever piping songs forever new."
1909-10	Studies pediatrics in Leipzig; leaves to visit Pound in London and his brother in Rome. Returns to open practice in Rutherford.
1912	December 12: marries Florence Herman.
1913	*The Tempers.* London: Elkin Mathews. 32 pp. Again costs the poet $50.00. Nineteen poems, including four love songs translated from the Spanish. Publication arranged by Ezra Pound.
1913-14	Joins an informal group of poets under the leadership of Walter Arensberg and Alfred Kreymborg which publishes *The Glebe* (ten numbers, including "Des Imagistes").
1914	First encounters with the poets of the *Others* movement, including Marianne Moore, through Kreymborg.
1915-19	Contributes to *Others*, along with Stevens, Pound, Eliot, and Moore.

The *Chronology of Important Dates* was compiled by Richard A. Macksey and is used here with his kind permission.

1917   *Al Que Quiere! A Book of Poems.* Boston: The Four Seas Company. 87 pp. Costs the poet another $50.00. Marks the start of his metric experiments.

1920   *Kora in Hell: Improvisations.* Boston: The Four Seas Company. 86 pp. Frontispiece by Stuart Davis.

1920-23   With Robert McAlmon edits the first *Contact.*

1921   *Sour Grapes.* Boston: The Four Seas Company. 78 pp.

1923   *Spring and All.* Dijon: Contact Publishing Co. 93 pp. Poems interspersed with "disturbed" prose.
            The. Great American Novel. Paris: Three Mountains Press. 79 pp. A travesty: the heroine is a little Ford car—"she was very passionate—a hot little baby."
            Go Go. Manikin No. 2 (pamphlet). New York: Monroe Wheeler. 22 pp.

1924   Travels in Europe: Paris, Rome, Vienna.

1925   *In the American Grain.* New York: Albert & Charles Boni. 235 pp.

1927   Trip to Europe; Mrs. Williams and sons stay on for school year.

1928   *A Voyage to Pagany.* The Macaulay Company. 338 pp. Dedicated to "the first of all of us, my old friend Ezra Pound." Written in Rutherford while Mrs. Williams and their two sons were in Europe.

1929   *Last Nights of Paris,* by Philippe Soupault. Translated from the French by William Carlos Williams. New York: The Macaulay Company (Transatlantic Library). 230 pp.

1931   Wins Guarantors Prize from *Poetry* magazine.

1932   With Nathaniel West edits revival of *Contact.*
            The Cod Head. San Francisco: Harvest Press. 4 pp. Title poem.
            A Novelette and Other Prose. Toulon: TO Publishers. 126 pp.
            The Knife of the Times and Other Stories. Ithaca, N. Y.: The Dragon Press. 164 pp. First book of short stories.

1934   *Collected Poems 1921-1931.* Preface by Wallace Stevens. New York: The Objectivist Press. 134 pp. Published by Louis Zukofsky "and the gang."

1935   *An Early Martyr and Other Poems.* New York: The Alcestis Press. 68 pp. Dedicated to John Coffey (a young radical).

1936   *Adam and Eve and The City.* Peru, Vermont: Alcestis Press. 69 pp. *The First President.* Libretto for an Opera. Published in *American Caravan,* a yearbook edited by Alfred Kreymborg, Lewis Mumford, and Paul Rosenfeld.

1937   *Two Drawings and Two Poems.* With William Zorach. (Pamphlet No. 1.) [N. Y.]: Stovepipe Press. [8] pp.
            White Mule. A Novel. Norfolk, Conn.: New Directions. 293 pp.

1938   *Life Along the Passaic River.* Norfolk, Conn.: New Direc-

tions. 201 pp. Continuation of the stories in *The Knife of the
Times*. Most of the stories had been published in Fred Miller's
Blast.
*The Complete Collected Poems of William Carlos Williams
1906-1938*. Norfolk, Conn.: New Directions. 317 pp.

1940   *In the Money*. Part II of *White Mule*. Norfolk, Conn.: New
        Directions. 382 pp.

1941   *The Broken Span*. (The Poet of the Month, No. 1.) Norfolk,
        Conn.: New Directions. 32 pp. Poems old and new.

1942   *Trial Horse No. 1 (Many Loves)*. An Entertainment in Three
        Acts and Six Scenes. Published in *New Directions 1942 Year
        Book*.

1944   *The Wedge*. Cummington, Mass.: Cummington Press. 109 pp.

1946   *Paterson, Book One*. New York: New Directions.
        First Act (a reissue by New Directions of the two parts of
        White Mule).

1947   Lectures at the University of Washington (returns in 1950).

1948   *Paterson, Book Two*. New York: New Directions.
        A Dream of Love. A Play in Three Acts and Eight Scenes.
        New York: New Directions. 107 pp.
        The Clouds. Cummington, Mass.: The Cummington Press.
        64 pp. Published jointly with the Wells College Press.

1949   *The Pink Church*. Columbus, Ohio: Golden Goose Press.
        Selected Poems. Introduction by Randall Jarrell. New York:
        New Directions. 140 pp.
        Paterson, Book Three. New York: New Directions.

1950   *A Beginning on the Short Story*. Yonkers: Alicat Press. 23 pp.
        Make Light of It: Collected Stories. New York: Random
        House. 342 pp.
        The Collected Later Poems. New York: New Directions. 240
        pp.

1951   *The Collected Earlier Poems*. New York: New Directions. 467
        pp.
        Paterson, Book Four. New York: New Directions.
        Autobiography. New York: Random House. 402 pp.
        Suffers first stroke; retires from medical practice.

1952   *The Build-Up*. A Novel. New York: Random House. 335 pp.
        More fiction drawn from Mrs. Williams' family history.

1954   *The Desert Music and Other Poems*. New York: Random
        House. 90 pp.
        Selected Essays. New York: Random House. 342 pp.
        A Dog and the Fever. A perambulatory Novella by Don
        Francisco de Quevedo. Translated by William Carlos Williams
        and Raquel Hélène Williams. Hamden, Conn.: The Shoe
        String Press. 96 pp.

1955   A reading tour of colleges across the country.
        Journey to Love. New York: Random House. 87 pp.

1957   *The Selected Letters of William Carlos Williams.* Edited by John C. Thirlwall. New York: McDowell, Obolensky, Inc. 347 pp.
        The Lost Poems of William Carlos Williams. Collected by John C. Thirlwall in *New Directions 16.*

1958   *Paterson, Book Five.* New York: New Directions.
        I Wanted to Write a Poem. Boston: Beacon Press. 99 pp.
        Forced to decline invitation to Bollingen Poetry Festival at the Johns Hopkins University by another cerebral accident.

1959   *Yes, Mrs. Williams: A Personal Record of My Mother.* New York: McDowell, Obolensky. 144 pp.

1961   *The Farmers' Daughters.* The Collected Stories. New York: New Directions. 375 pp.
        Many Loves and Other Plays. New York: New Directions. 437 pp.

1962   *Pictures from Brueghel and Other Poems.* New York: New Directions. 184 pp.

1963   Receives the Pulitzer Prize for *Pictures from Brueghel.*
        The Collected Later Poems. Revised Edition. New York: New Directions. 276 pp.
        March 4: dies in Rutherford, N.J.
        Paterson. Including Notes for Book Six. New York: New Directions. 284 pp.

Notes on the Editor and Authors

J. HILLIS MILLER, the editor of this volume, is Professor of English at Johns Hopkins. His *Poets of Reality* includes a study of Williams' work.

EZRA POUND, one of the century's most influential poets, first met William Carlos Williams when they were students together at the University of Pennsylvania.

MARIANNE MOORE, distinguished poetess and another of Williams' early associates, was the recipient of some of his important letters.

KENNETH BURKE, one of America's most important literary critics, was another long-time friend of Williams.

WALLACE STEVENS, celebrated poet, was another of Williams' early acquaintances.

YVOR WINTERS, well-known poet and critic, is Professor of English at Stanford University. Further pages on Williams are to be found in his *In Defense of Reason*.

LOUIS L. MARTZ, who is Professor of English at Yale University, is best known for *The Poetry of Meditation*, but has published many essays on modern poetry.

HUGH KENNER has published numerous books on modern literature. He is Professor of English at the University of California, Santa Barbara.

ROY HARVEY PEARCE is Chairman of the Department of Literature at the University of California, San Diego. He is the author of many books and articles, the best-known being *The Continuity of American Poetry*.

SISTER M. BERNETTA QUINN is Professor of English at the College of Saint Teresa, Winona, Minnesota. A poetess and critic, she has published *The Metamorphic Tradition in Modern Poetry* and many other studies of modern literature.

DENIS DONOGHUE is a Fellow of King's College, Cambridge, and the author of *The Third Voice* and, more recently, *Connoisseurs of Chaos*, a study of American poetry.

RICHARD A. MACKSEY, poet, critic, and bibliophile, teaches in the Writing Seminars at Johns Hopkins.

KARL SHAPIRO, distinguished poet and critic, has written many important essays on modern literature. He now teaches at the University of Nebraska.

ROBERT LOWELL, one of the best living American poets, has published several books of poetry, among them *Lord Weary's Castle* and *Life Studies*.

ROBERT CREELEY, a leader of the Black Mountain group of poets, and the author of *For Love, The Island,* and *The Gold Diggers,* lives in New Mexico.

CID CORMAN, editor of *Origin* and proprietor of the Origin Press, has published a number of volumes of verse and translations. His work as editor, poet, and critic testifies to Williams' influence on present-day writing in America.

THOM GUNN was educated at Trinity College, Cambridge. He is Assistant Professor of English at the University of California, Berkeley, and has published *Fighting Terms, The Sense of Movement,* and *My Sad Captains*.

Selected Bibliography

Blackmur, R. P., *Language as Gesture*. New York: Harcourt, Brace & World, Inc., 1952.

Bogan, Louise, *Achievement in American Poetry, 1900-1950*. Chicago: Henry Regnery Co., 1951.

Brinnin, John Malcolm, *William Carlos Williams*. University of Minnesota Pamphlets on American Writers, No. 24. Minneapolis: University of Minnesota Press, 1963.

Burke, Kenneth, "The Methods of William Carlos Williams," *The Dial*, LXXXII (February 1927), 94-98.

Cambon, Glauco, *The Inclusive Flame: Studies in American Poetry*. Bloomington, Indiana: Indiana University Press, 1963.

Cook, Albert, "Modern Verse: Diffusion as a Principle of Composition," *The Kenyon Review*, XXI (Spring 1959), 208-12.

Creeley, Robert, "The Fact of His Life," *The Nation*, CXCV (October 13, 1962), 224.

Deutsch, Babette, *Poetry in Our Time*. New York: Columbia University Press, 1956.

Flint, R. W., " 'I Will Teach You My Townspeople,' " *The Kenyon Review*, XII (Autumn 1950), 537-43.

Garrigue, Jean, "America Revisited," *Poetry*, XC (August 1957), 315-20.

Goodman, Paul, "Between Flash and Thunderstroke," *Poetry*, LXXXVII (March 1956), 366-70.

Gregory, Horace, "William Carlos Williams," *Life and Letters Today*, XXIV (February 1940), 164-76.

Hirschman, Jack, "William Carlos Williams," *Shenandoah*, XIV (Summer 1963), 3-10.

Hoffman, Frederick J., "Williams and His Muse," *Poetry*, LXXXIV (April 1954), 23-27.

Honig, Edward, "City of Man," *Poetry*, LXIX (February 1947), 277-84.

Jarrell, Randall, "The Poet and His Public," *Partisan Review*, XIII (September-October 1946), 488-500.

————, *Poetry and the Age*. New York: Alfred A. Knopf, Inc., 1953.

Kenner, Hugh, "Columbus Log-Book," *Poetry*, XCII (June 1958), 174-78.

———, "Dr. Williams Shaping His Axe," *Gnomon* (New York: Ivan Obolensky, Inc., 1958), pp. 55-66.

———, "To Measure Is All We Know," *Poetry*, XCIV (May 1959), 127-32.

Koch, Vivienne, *William Carlos Williams*. Norfolk, Conn.: New Directions Publishing Corporation, 1950.

Kreymborg, Alfred, *A History of American Poetry: Our Singing Strength*. New York: Tudor Publishing Co., 1934.

Lechlitner, Ruth, "The Poetry of William Carlos Williams," *Poetry*, LIV (September 1939), 326-35.

Levertov, Denise, "William Carlos Williams," *The Nation*, CXCVI (March 16, 1963), 230.

Martz, Louis, "Recent Poetry," *The Yale Review*, XXXVIII (Autumn 1948), 144-51.

Morgan, Frederick, "William Carlos Williams: Imagery, Rhythm, and Form," *The Sewanee Review*, LV (October-December 1947), 675-91.

Munson, Gorham B., "William Carlos Williams, A United States Poet," *Destinations: A Canvass of American Literature since 1900* (New York: J. H. Sears and Co., Inc., 1928), pp. 101-35.

Nash, Ralph, "The Use of Prose in *Paterson*," *Perspective*, VI (Autumn 1953), 191-99.

Pearce, Roy Harvey, "The Poet as Person," *The Yale Review*, XLI (March 1952), 421-40.

Pearson, Norman Holmes, "Williams, New Jersey," *The Literary Review*, I (Autumn 1957), 29-36.

Rexroth, Kenneth, "The Influence of French Poetry on American," *Assays* (Norfolk, Connecticut: New Directions Publishing Corporation, 1961), pp. 143-74.

———, "A Public Letter for William Carlos Williams' Seventy-fifth Birthday," *Assays* (Norfolk, Connecticut: New Directions Publishing Corporation, 1961), pp. 202-5.

Rosenfeld, Paul, *Port of New York*. New York: Harcourt, Brace & World, Inc., 1924.

Shapiro, Karl, *In Defense of Ignorance*. New York: Random House, Inc., 1952.

Solt, Mary Ellen, "William Carlos Williams: Idiom and Structure," *The Massachusetts Review*, III (Winter 1962), 304-18.

———, "William Carlos Williams: Poems in the American Idiom," *Folio*, XXV, No. 1 (1960), 3-28.

Spears, Monroe K., "The Failure of Language," *Poetry,* LXXVI (April 1950), 39-44.

Stearns, Marshall W., "Syntax, Sense and Sound in Dr. Williams," *Poetry,* LXVI (April 1945), 35-40.

Sutton, Walter, "Dr. Williams' *Paterson* and the Quest for Form," *Criticism,* II (Summer 1960), 242-59.

———, "A Visit with William Carlos Williams," *Minnesota Review,* I (Spring 1961), 309-24.

Thirlwall, John C., "William Carlos Williams' *Paterson:* The Search for the Redeeming Language—A Personal Epic in Five Parts," *New Directions 17* (1961), 252-310.

Wagner, Linda Welshimer, *The Poems of William Carlos Williams: A Critical Study.* Middletown, Connecticut: Wesleyan University Press, 1964.

Winters, Yvor, *In Defense of Reason.* New York: The Swallow Press and William Morrow and Co., Inc., 1947.

Zukofsky, Louis, "American Poetry 1920-30," *The Symposium* (January 1931), 60-84.

———, " 'The Best Human Value,' " *The Nation,* CLXXXVI (May 31, 1958), 500-502.

———, "An Old Note on William Carlos Williams," *The Massachusetts Review,* III (Winter 1962), 301-2.

The following issues of magazines have been devoted altogether or in part to Williams:

Briarcliff Quarterly, III, No. 11 (October 1946).

The Literary Review, I, No. 1 (Autumn 1957).

The Massachusetts Review, III, No. 2 (Winter 1962).

Perspective, VI, No. 4 (Autumn-Winter 1953).

Western Review, XVII, No. 4 (Summer 1953).